The New Dramatists
of Mexico
1967-1985

The New Dramatists of Mexico 1967-1985

Ronald D. Burgess

THE UNIVERSITY PRESS OF KENTUCKY

Publication of this book has been assisted
by a grant from Gettysburg College.

Copyright © 1991 by The University Press of Kentucky

Scholarly publisher for the Commonwealth,
serving Bellarmine College, Berea College, Centre
College of Kentucky, Eastern Kentucky University,
The Filson Club, Georgetown College, Kentucky
Historical Society, Kentucky State University,
Morehead State University, Murray State University,
Northern Kentucky University, Transylvania University,
University of Kentucky, University of Louisville,
and Western Kentucky University.

Editorial and Sales Offices: Lexington, Kentucky 40508-4008

Library of Congress Cataloging-in-Publication Data

Burgess, Ronald D.
    The new dramatists of Mexico, 1967-1985 / Ronald D. Burgess.
        p.   cm.
    Includes bibliographical references and index.
    ISBN 0-8131-1727-5 (acid-free paper)
    1. Mexican drama—20th century—History and criticism.   I. Title.
PQ7189.B8   1991
862—dc20   90-40023

This book is printed on acid-free paper meeting
the requirements of the American National Standard
for Permanence of Paper for Printed Library Materials. ∞

This book is dedicated to Professor George Woodyard, who helped me to begin, and who has always been there with help, encouragement, and good advice.

Contents

Acknowledgments

I would like to acknowledge the support given me by Gettysburg College during the production of this book. A series of Institutional Self-Renewal Grants made it possible for me to travel to Mexico and consult with playwrights in person. I would also like to thank all the writers who were so helpful. They were always willing to take the time to talk with me, to share copies of their books and manuscripts, and to supply me with names and phone numbers of other dramatists. Their generosity made the whole process much easier.

1. Introduction
The Formation of a Generation

The task of characterizing a literary generation is perhaps most wisely, or at least most easily, done after the fact. In the light of historical perspective one can define with some assurance the circumstances and events that unified and then held together a group of writers. Lost in this long view, however, are the immediacy and insights gained through personal contacts that exist only at the moment of formation. It is this immediacy and even a certain sense of urgency that lie behind this book. The urgency exists because the current group of young Mexican dramatists is something of a lost generation. For many years they were ignored by the Mexican public, by publishers, and by producers, and discouraged by the many obstacles placed before them during a period when the latest Broadway hits were preferred over Mexican plays. As a result most of the young playwrights of this new generation have remained almost completely anonymous. In fact, almost all of those who made up the original group eventually stopped writing drama, if for no other reason than economic necessity.

Happily, those early, discouraging days seem to be passing. There is more interest in plays by Mexicans and with good reason, since several of the newest dramatists have the potential to create an impact on theater not only in Mexico but in Spanish America in general. Suddenly many new playwrights are actively producing quality plays, they form a definable group, and they find themselves closer than ever to emerging as a potent force in Mexican literature. For these reasons now is the time to capture their first, formative years, to organize existing information, and to present the entire generation to the public in some sort of unified fashion. The purpose of the chapters that follow is to chronicle the early development of the most recent generation of Mexican dramatists, and to provide commentary on them, on their works, and on the principal elements that characterized them during the period from 1967 to 1985.

The designation of a new generation of writers and the selection of a nineteen-year span in which to situate them require some explanation. In the late sixties several young writers, still laboring in university workshops (primarily those of Emilio Carballido), began to write and then to publish and stage plays in university magazines and theaters. At the same time or shortly thereafter, other classes and workshops were begun under the direction of Luisa Josefina Hernández, Hugo Argüelles, Héctor Azar, and Vicente Leñero, to name only the most well-known. The "new generation," then, has in common a group of teachers and a point in time when they began to be active.

In the intervening years three separate actions have recognized more formally the existence of a group. First, Carballido published three anthologies of plays, *Teatro joven de México* (two collections with the same title) and *Más teatro joven de México*; in 1979, the Universidad Autónoma Metropolitana initiated a series of stage productions under the title of "La Nueva Dramaturgia"; and finally, one publishing house offered a series entitled "Serie Nueva Dramaturgia" devoted specifically to young Mexican dramatists. Clearly several diverse sectors and individuals perceived the presence of a cohesive group.

All of these perceptions can be substantiated somewhat more concretely by examining the birth dates of the writers under consideration. All of the dramatists studied here were born between 1939 and 1954, precisely the years indicated by José Juan Arrom in his *Esquema generacional de las letras hispanoamericanas* for the group due to come of age in the second half—that is, in 1969—of the "Generation of 1954." Arrom's scheme is discussed in more detail later in this chapter, but for now it need only be noted that the writers included were chosen on the basis of their activity and common characteristics; the coincidence of their birthdates appeared after the fact.

While the birthdates include a given set of writers, they exclude others, such as Carballido, Azar, and Leñero, who also wrote during the period mentioned. Their works are of interest as background for the more recent generation, but their previously established reputations as writers and their status as teachers exclude them from membership in the same group as their students.

These criteria provide an initial, if somewhat nebulous, framework for the existence of a group or generation. History provides another and perhaps more concrete clue. Mexican theater in the twentieth century has seen a series of high points and low points, beginning on the down cycle. Ruth Lamb and Antonio Magaña Esquivel, in their *Breve historia del teatro mexicano*, indicate that the early years of the century saw a decline in quality from previous years: "El auge que parecía haber alcanzado el teatro mexicano en cierto momento del último cuarto del siglo XIX decae en los primeros años del XX" (117). In his own *Medio siglo de teatro mexicano*, Magaña Esquivel says that prior to 1928, "El teatro mexicano no encontraba su asiento y los nuevos autores se hallaban desamparados" (28). In addition, a new "dramatic form"—the movies—began to attract the public that previously had formed the primary audience for theater. A new life for the theater, a "renovation," came in 1928, though, with the "Teatro de Ulises." Both the *Breve historia* and *Medio siglo* make mention of this important moment, and Margarita Mendoza López has detailed the rejuvenation of 1928 and the years thereafter in her *Primeros renovadores del teatro en México*. The year 1928 was clearly an important one in the development of Mexican theater.

The activity in the years that followed—activity initiated by Xavier Villaurrutia, Salvador Novo, Gilberto Owen, and Celestino Gorostiza, among others—brought Mexican theater into the mainstream of world drama. After some years, however, the force of the movement began to wane, and by the 1940s the theater found itself in another period of decline. Magaña Esquivel explains that, "Hacia 1947 el teatro, según las apetencias del público, era un espectáculo venido a menos" (*Medio siglo,*

99). As if in confirmation, in *Historia del teatro en México*, Yolanda Argudín entitles one section, "El teatro decae en los cuarentas." Lamb and Magaña Esquivel insist even more strongly, stating bluntly that, "el teatro mexicano entonces padece la crisis más amarga de su existencia" (126).

As all of these writers point out, though, this "crisis" came to an end in 1947, with the reorganization of the Instituto Nacional de Bellas Artes and its theater department. This new stimulus thrust Mexico into one of the most important periods of theater in its history (the 1950s and early 1960s) when more than two dozen dramatists were busy publishing and staging Mexican plays in unprecedented numbers. This period represents one of the high points in Mexican drama and includes what Argudín calls "la temporada de oro del teatro mexicano" (161).

This important stage of activity lasted into the mid-1960s, when once again Mexican theater assumed a new face—this time, Broadway's. Argudín explains: "El melodrama gana la guerra en la taquilla. Se importan sumisa y minuciosamente todos los éxitos, musicales o no, del teatro de Broadway" (172). Mexican drama slowly fell out of favor, and the resulting lack of interest in staging such plays at precisely that moment produced an almost fatal impact on the generation of writers that was just beginning to express itself. Argudín details the effects on the members of the pending generation: "En México difícilmente encontraron nuevas oportunidades, para vivir tuvieron que dedicarse a diferentes actividades y no a la teatral. De aquí el desmembramiento de lo que prometía un futuro en el teatro mexicano" (197).

The force of this blow fell on the new group especially, but all of those involved in theater were concerned, as evidenced by a series of conferences held during the mid-1960s, the texts of which were gathered into a book, *¿Qué pasa con el teatro en México?* The answers, given in more than a dozen presentations by some of the most important figures in Mexican theater, are overwhelmingly negative and pessimistic. Specifically, to the question posed by the title of the series (and later of the book), came responses such as: "En este momento suele resultar muy desolador estudiar una cartelera mexicana y ver lo que se está poniendo" (Luis Guillermo Piazza, 37); "no pasa nada, o pasa muy poco" (Seki Sano, 45). And, as summarized by Héctor Azar: "Una cartelera diaria raquítica en la que predominan las reiteradas chabacanerías del teatro comercial. Un teatro oficial lleno de limitaciones como increíbles problemas que poco o nada tienen que ver con la naturaleza íntima del teatro . . . Pocos, muy pocos autores nacionales y menos, muchos menos, los de calidad. Generaciones de artistas que se pierden o se quedan flotando entre la inactividad o la concesión máxima" (157).

Such seeming desolation recalls to a great extent the conditions previously attributed to the mid-1920s and the mid-1940s. This brief historical overview underscores the fact that in this century Mexican theater suffered a crisis every twenty years, and that in each case a new generation appeared and rescued the theater, first in 1928 and then in 1947. The suggestion, based on this pattern, is that another new generation was due at the end of the 1960s.

Taken together these various ingredients—the presence of a group of young dramatists, the activity engendered by them, Arrom's generational scheme, and the historical cycle—point to the appearance of a generation at almost exactly the period under consideration. As to the selection of a specific year that would mark the beginning of the new generation, there are three possibilities. Artistically the choice could well be 1967, the year in which the two most important writers of the generation's first wave began to publish. In that year Oscar Villegas and Willebaldo López wrote and/or staged six plays (Villegas's first play is from 1966). Their work grew to a great extent out of workshops directed by members of the previous generation, and follows by exactly twenty years the initiation of the Bellas Artes movement, the activity that launched the careers of those who taught in the 1980s.

A second possibility might be structured around the scheme proposed by Arrom. He describes a division of literary generations into thirty-year intervals, beginning with the year 1474. Each successive period represents the most productive years of those born during the preceding thirty years. Carrying this scheme up to the present day, the year 1954 marks the beginning of the generation of "Reformists," which extends until 1984. At times Arrom supplements his own formulation with that of José

Ortega y Gasset and divides his thirty-year periods into two fifteen-year subgroups, "dos etapas," explaining that, "esas promociones son algo así como las dos vertientes de una misma ola" (Arrom, 25). The first subgroup of the "Reformistas" consists of writers born between 1924 and 1939 who reached maturity between 1954 and 1969. These dramatists revitalized Mexican theater in the 1950s, and Arrom's scheme reflects their appearance very accurately. The second subgroup consists of those playwrights born between 1939 and 1954 and whose maturity spanned the years 1969 to 1984—the generation under consideration here. Arrom's divisions, then, would suggest 1969 as the year that inaugurates the new group.

The third possibility that presents itself is to a great extent political, and relates to a general upheaval in 1968. That year saw riots in Paris, the demonstrations in Chicago at the Democratic national convention, the movements surrounding the Olympic Games in Mexico City, and perhaps most importantly for Mexican dramatists, the violence of Tlatelolco. While relatively few playwrights have dealt directly with the latter events, they had an impact, and by looking carefully, one can see their effects behind the ideas of a large number of recent plays.

A choice among one of the three possibilities really becomes a matter of personal preference and inclination. The importance of the events of 1968 and their influence on the dramatists might well give that year prominence in the search for a moment that defines the generation. In a practical sense, though, it is more convenient to mark the period between 1967 and 1985 because those years frame what might be called the "gestation period" for the generation. The activity of Oscar Villegas, one of the most important playwrights in the group, reflects very well the common pattern found among his contemporaries. He was one of the first to begin writing, but by 1973 a combination of economic and artistic considerations had forced him away from the theater, and his next play did not appear in print until 1985. Somewhat encouraged by a press and public that finally seemed receptive to plays by young Mexican dramatists, he (along with several others who formed the first wave of the generation) again became interested in writing. The frame established by the birth and "rebirth" of one of the premier dramatists of this generation provides a convenient set of limits to mark the formation of what could be one of Mexico's most important generations of play-wrights.

The current generation has developed in three distinct and readily definable stages. The writers in the original group, the first wave of the generation, produced the vast majority of their plays between 1967 and 1973. At that point most of them turned away from writing drama and began to devote their energies to other endeavors. The period from 1974 to 1978 delimits a marked pause in the overall production by young dramatists. Of 215 plays written between 1967 and 1985, only 39, or about 18 percent of the total, were written in the five-year period of near dormancy, and fully one-fourth of those come from only one writer, Gerardo Velásquez. By 1979, the public, publishers, and producers finally were beginning to show at least passing interest in the works of the younger playwrights. That year marks the beginning of a virtual explosion of plays, primarily by a new group of writers, but more recently by some of the original group who are attracted by the positive interest.

The first wave of plays (1967-1973) was, in great part, drama of social protest written from the viewpoint of the young. In most cases the generation gap played an important part in the dramatic conflict, and the perspective was inevitably from the teen-age side of the separation. The characters reacted against the unfair treatment imposed on them by parents, teachers, government, and society in general. Malkah Rabell goes so far as to claim that, "Los jóvenes dramaturgos mexicanos llegaban a los festivales y concursos con la declaración mayoritaria: 'Odio a mis padres y a mis maestros' " (204). Few of the plays extend to two acts, and the three-act form disappears altogether. The reduced length limits the number of conflicts, usually to just one, and the characters tend to fall into two principal categories: the young (mistreated, many times rebellious) and the old (authority figures). Many of the plays were written as part of student workshops and represent fairly narrow concerns and conflicts. Not surprisingly, the adult theater-going public did not readily embrace these plays that pilloried them unceasingly.

Oscar Villegas and Willebaldo López are two important exceptions. Villegas, acknowledged all along as one of the preeminent writers of the generation, stands out in particular because his plays rarely dealt with the theme of the generation gap. His works focused on society at large and while his contemporaries tended to work in a realistic mode, his style more closely resembles that of the absurdists. His fragmented, stylized form and thematic depth are reflected to some extent in the plays written in the second wave of the generation.

López's plays offer a less restricted social protest than that of the young against the old: he pitted people against the system, and, like Villegas, anticipated what was to come. While other writers concerned themselves with the troubles of the young, López eventually began to look back into Mexico's history and culture, thus evoking a broader sense of the nation and at the same time delving into questions that touched peoples and nations other than Mexico. López was the first member of the generation to work with this theme that became so prominent in the second wave. First, however, there was the five-year pause.

Discouragement and economic considerations caused almost all of those who made up the initial force of the generation to stop writing plays by 1973. Despite their best efforts, the writers almost always encountered obstacles as they tried to bring new works to a public outside of the university. López wrote two more, and there are other scattered examples, but for the most part, activity ceased. The most notable exception is Gerardo Velásquez, who wrote his first play near the end of the first period, then almost single-handedly carried on during the time of decline. Of the thirty-nine plays that appeared during those years, he wrote ten, which means that, aside from his work, the generation as a whole only produced twenty-nine plays in five years, just 13 percent of the total produced by this group of writers between 1967 and 1985.[1]

In Velásquez's early plays he concentrated on human relations in general, many times from the point of view of the female character, and often in a small-town setting. Later he turned to historical drama. Although he did not consciously follow the lead of Villegas and López, Velásquez did extend the use of important elements employed by both of them and he combined their best attributes. Like López he began to look to the past for his themes and, like Villegas, he expressed them in a fragmented structure. As in the case of his own predecessors, Velásquez did not influence later dramatists to any great extent, but he, like Villegas and López, did anticipate the type of play that so many others would soon be writing.

The decline in production during the five years that lie at the center of this nineteen-year period helps to characterize the development of the generation. Carballido perhaps more than anyone worked actively and continuously throughout the period to advance the cause of the younger writers, and the three volumes of *Teatro joven* that he edited have contributed enormously to the current increase in interest. The first volume of *Teatro joven de México* appeared in 1973, just before the first year of the five-year decline, and promptly disappeared. Foreign plays, and especially Broadway hits, were still the rage at that point, and there was little interest in Mexican plays.

The second attempt, also entitled *Teatro joven de México*, met with more success, so much so in fact that it went into several printings. Its appearance in 1979 corresponds to the end of the dry period and presaged the increased activity since then. The second wave of playwrights includes more dramatists, more plays, more publications, more performances, and in general more attention than that enjoyed by the first wave. The increased opportunities produced a more optimistic group of writers. Their relative success allowed them to see their work on stage and in print, thereby providing them with experience that many of the first dramatists in the generation never acquired. This important advantage allowed the more recent writers to consider their plays from a new perspective and may well have been a contributing factor toward a shift in thematic focus: away from the problems of the generation gap and toward an examination of Mexico's history, culture, folklore, and society.

These new plays show more thematic depth and more conscious use of formal elements than most of the dramas that preceded them, with the exception of those by Villegas. Compared to previous works, the more recent plays are also "popular." The "Nueva Dramaturgia" series sponsored by the Universidad Autónoma Metropolitana was created exclusively for the young playwrights, and new Mexican plays began to be premiered not only in Mexico City, but in Jalapa and various other cities both in and out of Mexico. The public responded in part because the "foreign-theater-is-better" craze seemed to be passing, but also because the playwrights provided works of quality with a variety of themes.

Thematically and structurally the new dramatists represented a marked contrast from the playwrights who wrote in the 1950s and early 1960s. Plays by Luis G. Basurto, Wilberto Cantón, Jorge Ibargüengoitia, Sergio Magaña, and Rafael Solana dominated Mexico's stages during those years. Theirs was basically a realistic, traditional drama concerned in many cases with interpersonal relationships. They tended to provide social commentary rather than social protest, and they enjoyed commercial success with their work. Perhaps more socially conscious and more technically daring were those such as Emilio Carballido who became the teachers for the younger writers. Carballido still leads workshops, edits anthologies, promotes new talent, and maintains the steady production of plays that he began in the early 1950s. Luisa Josefina Hernández, Vicente Leñero, Hugo Argüelles, and Héctor Azar have also taught and led workshops. Leñero turned to drama in the late 1960s; he, Carballido, Maruxa Vilalta, and even Carlos Fuentes broke out of the traditional mold, and their themes, language, and form are reflected in the work of the younger writers.

Plays such as Carballido's *Ceremonia en el templo del tigre*, Vilalta's *Nada como el piso 16*, and Fuentes's *El tuerto es rey* examine the effects of corruption, the desire for power and control, and the physical and mental violence that accompany them. Other plays such as *Yo también hablo de la rosa* (Carballido) and *La carpa* (Leñero) explore the question of reality—what constitutes reality and who makes the determination? The same two writers employed characters and incidents from Mexico's history, as in *Tiempo de ladrones* (Carballido) and in Leñero's examples of *teatro documental*. The language in these and other plays ranges from realistic (*Tiempo de ladrones* and most of *La mudanza* [Leñero]) to absurdist and stylized (Fuentes, Vilalta, Azar). Many of these writers' plays include criticism of the power structure, and that is the most obvious point of contact between their works and those of their students.

It is these students who form the basis for this book, and

Villegas and López were two of the most important. Since they initiated the work of the young generation it is only proper to begin a study with them. The first wave of the generation included a relatively small number of other writers. Their work is discussed before turning to that of a still smaller group of writers who continued or began to write in the early 1970s, approximately the same time that Velásquez began to publish plays. Two other dramatists, Carlos Olmos and Jesús González Dávila (the latter forming a part of the original group) produced plays both before and after the five-year period of decline, and their work is discussed separately.

The writers who comprise the second wave of the generation are most easily grouped by common themes. Sabina Berman and Tomás Espinosa were concerned with history, culture, folklore, and the question of what comprises reality. Oscar Liera and Victor Hugo Rascón Banda focused on society and criticized its inequalities and those groups seemingly intent on maintaining the social and economic divisions. Eighteen more dramatists with a wide variety of approaches but a somewhat less sustained production are discussed in a separate chapter. By way of conclusion, the frame on this generation can be completed by returning to the latest work by Oscar Villegas, a play that conveniently leads to a summary of the works produced by this potentially important generation of Mexican dramatists.

The analytic methods used to explore the works vary from chapter to chapter. The diversity represented by writers such as Villegas, López, Olmos, González Dávila, Berman, Espinosa, Liera, and Rascón Banda calls for an equally diverse critical approach. In one case myth criticism may serve to provide the best insights into a playwright's work; in another, structuralism, semiotics, or formalism might prove more profitable. As a result, a rather eclectic collection of methods is used throughout the commentary that follows.

It might also be noted that the focus is on young Mexican playwrights, so there is scant mention of works by their contemporaries in other Latin American countries. Although these writers seem to have relatively little in common with dramatists in Mexico, there are a few shared elements, beginning with the term used to identify them. Carlos Pacheco refers to "teatro joven" when writing about recent theater in Argentina. Speaking of the young Argentine writers' dilemma he describes the same obstacles that confronted Mexican dramatists: "Entonces las salas no se ceden porque quienes las piden son los jóvenes, la prensa no los considera porque son jóvenes, el público no arriesga el pago de una entrada porque son jóvenes" (122). Edith Pross explains the results of such attitudes: "At the end of the seventies, Argentine theatre scholars were ready to lament the lack of emerging new talent on the stages of local theatres" (83). These concerns are similar to those expressed in Mexico. Furthermore, Roberto Ramos-Perea dates the "nueva dramaturgia puertorriqueña" from 1968 (61-62), as does Azparren Giménez when referring to Venezuela's most recent generation of playwrights (80).

Despite these similarities, in general the direction taken and the methods employed by Mexican playwrights differ substantially from those undertaken in other countries. In *El nuevo teatro latinoamericano: Una lectura histórica*, Beatriz Rizk lists the following influences on that theater: "El teatro político-épico de Piscator, el teatro épic-dialéctico de Brecht, el teatro grotesco de Pirandello, el teatro sociológico de O'Neil y más tarde de Miller" (35). To that list might be added absurdist theater, Artaud's theater of cruelty, and alternatives such as the "Living Theater." Examples of most of these can be found only rarely, if at all, in new Mexican drama. Some works by Villegas, González Dávila, Olmos, and Pilar Campesino exhibit absurdist touches; but the only real influence is in the psychological element involved in concerns about the generation gap.

In most of Latin America, theater groups and *creación colectiva* are of some importance. La Candelaria and TEC in Colombia and ICTUS in Chile have been influential for years, as has the "Teatro Abierto" in Argentina. Mexico has no groups of comparable stature. Similarly, collective theater has not made any significant inroads into new Mexican drama. Generally there has been much less experimentation with alternative forms of creating and staging plays in Mexico than in other countries in Latin America or Europe. And while many contemporary Mexican plays express discontent with the social and political situation, there exists no radical political agenda, as evidenced, for example, by the lack of plays about Tlatelolco. There is certainly not the equivalent of what Robert Morris calls Peru's "over-zealous revolutionary theatre" (61).

Conditions in Mexico have contributed to these differences. For example, Enrique Buenaventura's interest in *creación colectiva* helped to guide theater in Colombia, but Emilio Carballido, arguably the most influential force in Mexican theater led Mexico in other directions. The relative political stability in Mexico created circumstances different from those in many other parts of Latin America—corruption is one thing; violence and suppression are quite another. There are fewer cases of "official" censorship in Mexico than in other countries (José Agustín's *Círculo vicioso* is one example); economic censorship is far more prevalent. Finally, Mexican playwrights have never been forced into exile, as has happened in Chile for example.

Thus recent Mexican theater progressed by its own rhythm and rules. The dramatists were no less politically or socially conscious than their contemporaries in other countries, they just had a different set of circumstances from which to begin, not the least of which was the Mexican Revolution and its promise. When Mexicans look to their past for an understanding of their present, they have that revolution to consider since it is such an intimate part of their heritage. Mexico's past, the hopes that grew from the Revolution, and how those hopes evolved became prominent among the themes of the newest generation of Mexican playwrights, those who constitute Mexico's "Nueva Dramaturgia."

2. The Early Years
Villegas and López

It is generally accepted that there is a difference between "drama" and "theater." In "Aproximación semiológica a la 'escena' del teatro del Siglo de Oro español," José María Diez Borque makes the distinction in terms of two texts, A and B: "*Texto a*: el texto de la obra. Coincide con los otros géneros literarios, aunque con particularidades propias. *Texto b*: el texto escénico. Da especificidad teatral" (53). According to Diez Borque, the communication process of Text A has a linguistic base, and in Text B the base is visual-acoustic (53). These characteristics help to differentiate the works of the first two writers in the newest generation of Mexican theater: Oscar Villegas focuses on the linguistic aspect, and Willebaldo López emphasizes the visual.

Almost all of the first wave of playwrights in this generation participated in the classes and workshops of writers like Emilio Carballido and Luisa Josefina Hernández, and thus they share a common background. They also shared the early struggle to bring their work to the public—the theater-goers who, at the time, were more interested in foreign plays than in Mexican ones, and the theater owners and managers who were only too happy to oblige them. From the small group of new dramatists who managed to make themselves known (through small-time publications and, in many cases, shoestring productions of their works), three stood out very early and achieved what, at the time, had to be considered success. Even though Carballido supported the whole group, by helping its members to get their plays staged and by publishing them in the first of the *Teatro joven de México* series, José Agustín, Villegas, and López managed to attract the most attention.

Agustín managed to publish and stage two plays, one notable for its inventiveness and the other for its notoriety,[1] but his dramatic production is limited to those two works and one other short piece. He belongs only to the fringe of the generation, a judgment that is confirmed by the lack of any further dramatic activity by him. Villegas, on the other hand, continued to write plays until economic necessity forced him into other endeavors for several years. He not only received critical attention in published articles, but he was also mentioned by his peers as perhaps the most talented dramatist of the generation. His talent notwithstanding, Villegas's works were staged only infrequently, and then very badly. Some of the reasons become obvious during the discussion of his plays. López's success came directly from the stage. Several of his plays were produced in "name" theaters in Mexico City, enjoyed relatively long runs, and received numerous awards. Such attention for a Mexican playwright was almost unheard of at that time.

Villegas and López took very different approaches to drama, although the ideas communicated through their work have elements in common. Villegas's plays stress the literary text. He subordinates plot, strict dramatic structure, and characterization to the power of language. One watches his plays as if they were scenes illuminated by strobe lights. The ideas flash by in bits and pieces, embedded in language play and layered images, and challenge the spectators or readers to participate in the formation of those ideas. In comparison, López's work is more readily understood because his plays depict everyday life realistically. The people in his first plays are readily recognizable recreations of the friends, neighbors, and family members of the audience; later, they are characters from Mexico's history and culture—somewhat more removed in time, but still immediately familiar.

Villegas's and López's plays may differ in style, but thematically the two writers aimed at the same target: the negative effects societal conditions have on those who must endure them. Both depicted the world as a play consisting of dramatists and characters (dramatized). According to Villegas, one of society's primary functions is the creation of victims. López saw much the same result, but his plays focused more on a search for causes. In both cases the suggestion is that some people are able to create the reality around them, but that for others it has already been created and they are condemned (or content) to suffer in the daily dramas that are established for them. Villegas looked at the state of those who are dramatized (that is, victimized), and López searched for the dramatists.

Oscar Villegas

Villegas's first seven plays exhibit a strong stylistic and thematic consistency: linguistic and imagistic density, and a focus on society. Since his plays are not rooted in a specifically Mexican culture, the society they depict, over and over again, can exist anywhere. It is composed of twisted and many times perverted individuals who are trapped in a circle that forces them alternately to victimize and to be victimized. They seem to need others, but that need is the very element that drags them into the circle from which they cannot escape. Those who are lonely and isolated need others for love and companionship; what they get instead is victimization and abuse. Once they find themselves in that position, they must assert themselves to escape, but the resulting self-assertion almost inevitably involves using and victimizing others—actions that again isolate them and return them to the originating point on the circle. Since all members of society alternate between these two roles, the individual becomes a meaningless, shadowy figure in a constantly shifting scene. George Woodyard reached the same conclusion in "El teatro de Oscar Villegas: experimentación con la forma." He wrote, "[Villegas] pinta una sociedad con parámetros estrechos y pervertidos que no respeta los derechos del hombre, o que lo explota en su afán de convertirle en algo que no es, y que a veces hace que se destruya a sí mismo" (41). He then added, "En vez de alcanzar la felicidad, queda convertido en otra cara anónima en un mar de seres sin identidad propia" (41). Villegas looked at society, and what he saw was not pretty.

The picture of that society does not come to the audience easily. Structurally, Villegas's plays are highly fragmented. The thirty-eight pages that comprise *La paz de la buena gente*, for example, contain thirty-four scenes. The effect is similar to that produced by absurdist theater, and the language, especially in the first plays, also tends to have an absurdist flavor. As Martin Esslin explained, in absurdist drama "the total action of the play, instead of proceeding from point A to point B, as in other dramatic conventions, gradually builds up the complex pattern of the *poetic image* that the play expresses. The spectator's suspense consists in waiting for the gradual completion of this pattern which will enable him to see the image as a whole" (366). With Villegas, however, spectators do not wait as much as they participate—at least if they plan to make sense of the pattern that unfolds.

The structure and language, together with the intense focus on a small group of characters who represent the whole of any given society, present a stylized picture that is very close to Victor Shklovsky's notion of "defamiliarization." According to Shklovsky, the purpose of "defamiliarization" is "to make objects 'unfamiliar,' to make forms difficult, to increase the difficulty and length of perception" (12). This Villegas certainly did. His plays are difficult and require work and thought to understand them. It is no wonder that, at a time when Mexico's theater public preferred popular Broadway musicals, Villegas's productions went nearly unnoticed. A brief look at some of his works helps to clarify this "strobe light drama"—plays that provide only brief flashes of a scene constantly in motion.

Villegas's first seven plays are consistent in their presentation of a vision of society and in their fragmented form, although the language becomes less stylized and more realistic and the characterization develops more fully in the sixth and seventh. *El renacimiento, La pira,* and *Santa Catarina* are representative of Villegas's view of society, where conflicts and tensions arise from fear and sex: the fear of discovery and of the loss of control, and the use and misuse of sexual contact.

El renacimiento presents one of the most common thematic concerns of the writers of this group: the problems of the generation gap. It is Villegas's only investigation of the topic, and he was less concerned with the friction between young and old than with the conflict between the traditional and the new—between uniformity and conformity on the one hand, and revolution on the other. The action takes place in an ultra-reactionary school; the head of the school and her beau appear in the first scene dressed in the costume and using the language of Spain's *Siglo de Oro*, although the time of the play's action is contemporary. A group of students calls for the inclusion in the curriculum of a seminar on "Inquietudes Comparadas" (24), probably as a balance for other courses, such as "Introducción al vestido, Cómo ser buenos ciudadanos en un discurso, táctica de expulsión de gases, y práctica del estornudo" (17). This group, the "Jóvenes de colores," is opposed by the more traditional "Jóvenes de gris" and urged on by four expelled students—Juan, Jorge, Pablo, and Ricardo, readily identifiable as the Beatles (John, George, Paul, and Ringo) even without the numerous Beatles' songs used as transitions between scenes.[2] The conflict finally evolves into a pitched battle between the conservative and the progressive elements in the play, and in the end the reactionary forces seem to win. The last scene presents some hope for reconciliation, but given the general tone of Villegas's other plays, that hope seems slim.

The sexual aspect dominates the actions of the characters in *La pira*. In fact, it is the primary motivation for the characters' actions, actions that produce the obvious consequences along with the attendant complication. The short play traces the development of a young girl who first rejects her boyfriend's advances, fearful of the reaction her father would have, and then gradually progresses to having sexual relations with a pair of boys, and finally with a whole group of them. Inevitably she becomes pregnant, and naturally none of the boys accepts the responsibility. In contrast to the archaic language, the wordplay, and the fragmented bits of conversation in *El renacimiento*, the characters in *La pira* use extremely colloquial language within a chronological structure.

The next step in this "realism" came with *Santa Catarina*, another foray into the world of sex. This time the focus is on homosexual relations, both sought after and forced, in an all-boys' military school. The first part of the play slowly reveals the web of emotions that entangles the main characters, including the unwanted advances forced on Manzanito by one of the older boys (Cuervo). When Manzanito finally runs away to escape the undesired attention, the whole network of relationships threatens to be revealed, and finally Cuervo runs away too, while the rest vow not to reveal any of the relations that have existed for so long.

While the primary action centers on the conflict between Manzanito and Cuervo and its effect on the other boys, this is just the superficial layer of the play. Although only two scenes among the play's twenty-two do not deal directly with the boys in the school and their problems, they add an important perspective. In one scene, significantly the first, a man finds a boy sleeping on the street and offers to take him home. With no other context, the action could be a gesture of kindness and compassion, but in the fourth scene, the man pushes the boy out his door with this admonition: "Aquí no vengas porque casi no estoy, cuando quieras verme vas al cine Victoria; lleva a tus amiguitos, más grandecitos que tú . . . Si me ves en la calle acompañado y no te hablo, tú también hazte el disimulado" (64-65). Within the context of the actions in the school, these two scenes take on a much more sinister tone. Aside from that, their effect is to pull the boys' actions into a much wider frame and to make the school simply a miniature of society, since the same things seem to go on both inside and outside the school. Much of what happens in the play occurs through the combination of outside influences and the boys' almost passive acceptance of their situation. The fact that their reality—the circumstances in which they live—is created for them introduces another one of the foundations of Villegas's work. It can be seen most clearly in two short plays.

Marlon Brando es otro is a short play (six pages) built from the story of a multiple murder that took place in an Arizona beauty shop in 1966.[3] The play has less to do with the killing, the killer, and Marlon Brando than with what the media and the public do with the situation. One series of scenes with the killer's family reveals what they perceive as his "real" personality, while a separate series, dominated by the public, establishes a totally different character for him. In this second personality the killer achieves celebrity status. When he finally appears, he simply reacts from both personalities, so that he effectively becomes the creation of those around him, a situation that he readily accepts. The message is that society creates its own victims, and the victims seem to accept their status (although some less willingly than others).

El señor y la señora offers a similar picture. The scene is a party celebrating the fiftieth wedding anniversary of the title characters. Again the play is extremely fragmented, with the unnamed characters drifting back and forth, providing bits and pieces of their conversations. The effect is very much like that of walking around at a party and hearing only fragments of what people are saying. The pieces eventually form a whole, however, since there is apparently only one real topic of interest: sex. Specifically, the characters spend their time discussing sadism, masochism, prostitution, infidelity, masturbation, impotence, Oedipal complexes, venereal diseases, homosexuality, and more, as these activities relate to their own personal situations. These practices appear to be the norm for these people. What is not the norm is the secretary one of the guests brings. The secretary, who does not engage in these sexual practices, soon finds herself the object of scorn. This distorted, satirical mirror of our own society demonstrates the need to create victims of those who do not conform to "acceptable behavior." The spectator's awareness of this develops slowly, however, because of the dramatic techniques employed by Villegas.

The same techniques are present in *La paz de la buena gente*, in which Villegas gives us the most complete picture of his slightly twisted society. There are no indications of any scenery, and the action is staged best on a darkened, empty stage—a piece of the world hanging alone in the midst of nothing. The isolation is reflected in the structure, the characters, the style, and the groups of people who inhabit this desolate place. Each of the thirty-four scenes, which range from one-quarter to two pages in length, reveals another fragment in the life of a character or set of characters. The characters themselves are faceless, indicated by number instead of name in the text. If one can speak of plot lines in this play, there are six, and the character or group of characters associated with each float in and out, seemingly arbitrarily, when their scenes come along. This structure is, as Esslin commented, "merely a device to express a complex total image by unfolding it in a sequence of interacting elements" (355). The language echoes the effect, as for example in the following piece of dialogue that begins the third fragment: "Yo. Tú. El. Nosotros. Vosotros. Ellos. ¿Quién más? ¿Nadie? Nadie existe, es el vacío a quien corresponda. Andamos de excursión para cada vez voltear y ver que alguien se queda. Nos encontramos unos, todos entre otros. He perdido la ocasión que me condujo aquí, y no es el final . . . la última salida. Mis hermanos duermen sin prisa y hay otros puentes . . . hace tanto tiempo que salí de viaje . . . "(15). The vocabulary—"nadie, vacío, perdido, final, última, salí"—underscores the speaker's loneliness.

The total image in this case is a society based on "Siluetas" who are at once faceless, vicious, and utterly empty. They wander in occasionally, muttering words, but saying nothing at all. At various times, one character (number 1) asks them for information, but nothing they answer has any relation to his questions. Another character, apparently an aging prostitute, spends her time alone, talking to herself and reliving or creating a fantasy world of lovers. Yet another insists on her solitude, but only out of paranoia. Seemingly her loneliness has led to an uncontrollable fear of everyone else. The only thread of action with even a mildly positive note concerns the relationship between characters 2 and 4, which resembles something approaching poetic love. At the very least this woman and man communicate with each other, yet it seems to be to no avail since in the end she (#2) finds herself alone.

The one pair that achieves a semblance of unity is a couple that never manages to say anything meaningful. Their dialogue is composed of sounds, verb conjugations, the alphabet, the days of the week, and assorted questions and comments that relate only by chance. They and their "love" are as empty and meaningless as everything else in this vacuous society, and as a result they fit right in. In the end they are still together, telling each other stories ("Etcétera, etcétera, etcétera . . . " [47]), and sounding very much like the "Siluetas." That, in fact, may be why they "succeed": given that everyone else is alone, that these two remain together is something of an accomplishment. From another perspective, they have merely accepted the conformity forced on them by society; their reality has been constructed for them elsewhere, and they adopt it passively. Such is the society that Villegas depicts.

The same kind of place exists in much the same form in *At-lántida*, the last play Villegas wrote before turning to other crea-tive outlets. The fragmented structure is still there (thirty-three scenes) as well as the lack of real love, the solitude, the emphasis on sex, and the process of victimization. Only the language and the characterization have changed. The inhabitants of Atlántida, a poor neighborhood of Mexico City, use extremely colloquial language, and their individual personalities are more developed than those of characters in Villegas's earlier plays. Their situa-tion, however, is not. The story focuses on the attempts by Vir-ginia to become a famous dancer, to escape from her lower class *barrio*, and to find love. She settles for much less than she desires on all accounts. She loses one boyfriend after another, and she progresses from winning first place in a dance contest, to achiev-ing a degree of fame as a dancer, to working as a *rumbera* in a seedy club, and finally, after the destruction of the *barrio* in a flood, to an undetermined future.[4]

Like Villegas's other characters, Virginia, despite all her ef-forts, is left with nothing in the end. She is simply one more victim of an unrelenting society that insists on creating roles, usually false and empty, for its citizens. This pessimistic view is specifically Mexican only in the street language of the last few plays. The stylized presentation pulls the actions out of a specific place and leaves them to cast a shadow over any society that exhibits similar characteristics. Such universality lifts Villegas to a special place among his contemporaries. Although his plays may present an enormous challenge, anyone who meets it will have gained new insights from the experience.

Willebaldo López

Willebaldo López took a somewhat different tack. He stressed the Mexicanness of his characters, settings, and situations; placed them all in the context of absolute reality brought to the stage; then added a significant metatheatrical element for good measure. His plays, like those of Villegas, look at the condition of people within their society. Both are critical in their view, but where Villegas stylized to create intellectually intricate and im-agistic works, López used realism to produce clear, straightfor-

ward, Mexican dramas; where Villegas concentrated on victim-
izers and victimized, López depicted dramatists and dramatized.
His earliest plays were essentially metatheatrical dramas of social
criticism, but after the metatheatrical element grew so prevalent
that it made the criticism less effective, he changed the direction
of his writing and turned to historical and cultural themes.

López's dramatic techniques are consistent through all of his
plays: realism in language, character, and situation; an element
of spectacle associated with metatheater; and humor. Thematically, he suggested that society's problems exist, at least in part,
because of how people view each other and because of the continuing impact of Mexico's past on its present. Given his techniques, one conclusion that may be easily drawn is that life is
theater, and that people are dramatists, constantly trying to create the little plays that constitute their reality. The most proficient
manage to impose their dramas on those around them, and those
who are dramatized find themselves trapped, like the victims
in Villegas's plays, in scripts composed by others. Thus the two
writers saw the same problem in much the same way. The extra
step López took was to look for causes as well. To see the trajectory that he followed, it is best to look at his work in two
phases: first, the expression of the problem (specifically the state
of the poor), and then the search for causes (foreign exploitation
and the influence of the past). López's first three major plays
fall into the first category.

As its title suggests, *Los arrieros con sus burros por la hermosa
capital* is at least one part farce. The *arrieros* are poor country
people who think that the solution to their economic woes lies
in the city. The father and son go with their firewood-laden (and
invisible) burros to make money, but only encounter problems:
a series of stereotyped characters (foreigners living in Mexico,
tourists, a politician, a policeman, a group of lower class ruffians)
who either make fun of them, view them as curiosities, take
advantage of them, or mistreat them.

At the beginning the innocence and the down-home language
of the *arrieros* create a good deal of humor, but that tone soon
changes as the main characters lose their wood and the burros,
become discouraged, and return home in failure. The son, determined to make good, goes back to the city, and this time he

succeeds in earning money because he is willing to sell his dignity. He returns home again but arrives too late, because the father has already killed himself in shame. The son decides that the entire family should go to the capital to make their fortunes. Instead they lose their identity, dress up as Indians to dance on street corners, and turn to alcohol to drown their problems. In this case the culprits are the magical attraction of the beautiful capital as the answer to every problem, and the inhabitants, both foreign and native, who seem interested only in themselves and their own pleasure and advancement. The newcomers are not without fault, however, since they easily succumb to the drama of the city and are willing to become actors in the stereotypical roles assigned to them. The son is the prime example, with his *macho* attitudes, his steady drinking, and his determination to take on the education of his own children, even in the face of his own failure and lack of education.

Cosas de muchachos follows a similar pattern. It also served as López's contribution to the generation gap plays that were so common at the time. The two *muchachos* (a boy and a girl) escape from school, spend the day enjoying themselves, and eventually have to get married because the girl finds herself pregnant. Naturally the boy, who has no work experience, cannot get a job; he eventually begins to drink and finally dies in the street. His wife is forced to sell herself to a funeral director to pay for her husband's burial.

Although there are several characters in the play, there are only two actors. The reduced number of actors was partially a result of economics: plays with large numbers of participants were almost automatically rejected by producers because they would not earn enough money to be profitable. López turned this handicap into an advantage by having the characters take on other roles as they act out their thoughts. In the first act, for example, when the boy attempts to seduce the girl, she and the audience see him transformed into her father, who threatens to kill her if she becomes pregnant. Thus the boy is seen as a reflection of the father, which suggests that both possess the same violent, *macho* characteristics. This kind of visual imagery contributes to the dramatic effect of the play and at the same time expands its thematic base. *Cosas de muchachos* is not just a play about two young people who experience economic problems after they have to get married. It is a comment on the situation encountered by the young, on the economic problems that plague Mexico, and on human relations in a general sense—the "dramatization" of others.

López took the idea of dramatization and the effectiveness of his theatrical social criticism to its limit in *Vine, vi y mejor me fui,* a play in which he questioned his own dramatic process. The scene is an apartment in a poor section of the city during a wake for the family's baby. Before the play begins, the "Dramatist" comes out of the audience, arranges a few objects on stage, and indicates that everything is ready. The act that follows is merely a continuation of this reality. The Dramatist, who is a friend of the family and the baby's godfather, chats with family members and neighbors about their economic problems, their other neighbors, *machismo,* relationships, and life in general. Nothing really happens until the end of the act, when the husband and wife get into an argument and accidentally knock over the table with the baby's body. At this point, the Dramatist decides to insert an intermission: "¿Será aquí? . . . No sé. Pero . . . ¿En dónde? . . . ¿Cómo meter el intermedio? . . . Creo que . . . Bien. Sí, creo que puede ser aquí . . . Arbitrariamente . . . " (38).

The "characters" continue to talk during the intermission, directing their comments to the audience at times. Occasionally the mother asks if she can pick the baby up yet, until finally the Dramatist consents, and the second act begins. Since the Dramatist bases his plays on real life, the characters begin to tell him stories from their lives, but everyday life is not exciting enough. The Dramatist feels the need to make it more appealing, more "dramatic." López's first two plays were based on the concept of bringing real life directly to the stage, and this decision by the Dramatist undermines the foundation of those works— daily life is too boring. The solution, which occupies most of the second act, is to add more drama to the characters' lives to make them more interesting.

He uses the offstage noise of a fight between a neighbor and his wife to put the idea into action. While everyone else rushes out to stop the fight, the Dramatist begins to write. The stage directions indicate: "(*Se queda sentado frente a la mesa y empieza a*

*describir lo que ve, a escribir lo que imagina, a dudar, a preguntar al
público y a dejarse llevar posesionadamente del relato)"* (58). The Dramatist imagines that the neighbor's wife is killed, and when the
other characters return and inform him that she did indeed die,
he reacts with surprise: "*(Mirándolos con extrañeza)* ¿De veras la
mató?" (59). He has literally created reality. Since the stage actions up to this point have been real life brought to the stage,
the Dramatist's actions imply by extension that reality outside
the theater can also be created. He quickly realizes that his new
creation is too melodramatic, and since he wishes to use his plays
to communicate ideas and bring about change, he decides that
his methods—a simple transfer of life to the stage, embellished
or not—will not accomplish his goals. The results either lack
dramatic action or become melodramatic. Since life is drama and
drama is life, López the exterior dramatist came to the same
conclusion as his interior dramatist. He stopped writing plays
that reproduce contemporary life perfectly and turned to historical drama.

Commenting on the idea of interior duplication, which is one
of the techniques frequently used in these plays, Susan Wittig
explained: "The reduction of the dramatic situation to a framed,
refracted miniature of itself calls the audience's attention immediately to the stage, the *medium* of the dramatic presentation;
to the theatricality, rather than to the reality of the play, and
ultimately, as Abel asserts, to the artifice of life" (451).

The concept of interior duplication, López's frequent and extensive use of metatheater, and Lionel Abel's concept of life already theatricalized mesh nicely to resolve the dilemma in which
López and the Dramatist find themselves. A non-theatricalized
life (in this case the poor family whose baby died) is difficult to
bring to the stage, but to theatricalize it diverts attention to the
theatricality. The solution for López was to turn to already theatricalized life and characters: Benito Juárez, an Indian medicine
man, and *La Malinche*.

In *Yo soy Juárez* several students are preparing a play about
the hero, a play they plan to enter in a competition. Their idea
is to present the almost mythical character as a human being,
but the reaction against "belittling" such a national figure eventually forces them to give up their enterprise. Here López looked

at the detrimental effects of that kind of blind veneration of the past, which can determine how people think and act in the present. In fact, as the students rehearse the play, a series of scenes in the second act brings them to the point where they are no longer acting but are "living" the lives of their historical characters. The play suggests that the past has so dramatized the present that the present is already determined. The focus on the larger-than-life figure of Juárez establishes the theatrical element so important in López's plays and allows the drama to play itself out, realistically and metatheatrically, without having to resort to melodrama. At the same time, *Yo soy Juárez* educates (there is much historical information about Juárez) and establishes one possible reason for the problems that haunt the characters in López's society: the tyranny of the past, a past that imposes itself on the present and robs it of free choice.

With *Pilo Tamirano Luca* the notion of the creation of reality reappears in both figurative and literal form. The play essentially divides its characters into good and bad. Pilo, a Cora medicine man and healer, represents good, while the white people are the villains. Here reality is created in a number of ways. An ethnologist goes to a Cora village to do research for a book on Cora folklore. As Pilo tells him his life story, it is reenacted on stage, with younger actors taking the role of Pilo at first, and later with Pilo himself participating as both narrator and actor. Both his rise and his fall are depicted. His ascent is based on his abilities as a healer; his decline is based on a series of incidents that begin when he sells several sacred chants to the ethnologist. The play's structure proceeds on the basis of three aspects of this rise and fall: physical, spiritual, and material. As Pilo tells his story, he first narrates his birth (physical), followed by the discovery of his healing powers and his desire to perfect them (spiritual), and then the climb to his position as healer and medicine man. The materialistic aspect enters at this point, since those activities earn Pilo's living for him. It is also materialism that starts his downfall and brings about the repetition of the sequence, this time in reverse order. Selling the sacred chants is an extension of his materialism and causes his fall from power. His ensuing fatalism signals his spiritual death, which is followed closely by his physical death at the end of the play.

Opposition to Pilo and his power (and by extension to the Indians) comes from the white people. They wish to take advantage of the Cora nation for their own profit, although their true intentions are disguised behind the mask of progress for the villagers. The ethnologist criticizes such actions at the end of the play: "Los que venimos aquí, ya sea por carretera o avión, buscamos nuestro progreso, pero no el tuyo. Traemos progreso, progreso . . . Pero el progreso, ¿de quién?" (40). Essentially, then, the white people are attempting to dramatize the Indians, to create a new life for them.

This happens in its most literal sense when the ethnologist tries to tape-record a ceremony and forgets to press the record button. When the tribal elders discover that they cannot hear the recording, they assume that it is a sign of the gods' unhappiness with Pilo. His attempt to sell chants to the whites leads to Pilo's downfall.

Pilo himself is not above creating reality, either; in fact, it is his stock and trade. At one point, as he performs a ceremony, he "magically" produces a human bone. Later, when the ethnologist accuses him of deceit, he replies, "Yo no engaño. Sí se los saco [los huesos] a los muertos" (36). He goes on to explain, "Mira. Yo lo traigo aquí para sacárselos a los muertos. ¿Ves?" (36). In other words, it is all a question of one's point of view. He does produce bones and everyone accepts it as magic. Whether he acquired the bones previously or not is of consequence only to those who insist on a more scientific and "sophisticated" perspective. Reality can be created, for good or for bad, as long as there are those who allow themselves to be dramatized. In this case it is Pilo who takes advantage of that fact.

One of Mexico's premier dramatizations involves *la Malinche*, the subject of López's final play, *Malinche Show*. In it *la Malinche* is seen in the present, kept alive by an elaborate mechanism so that she can televise her "Malinche Show." Every day she urges all Mexicans to continue selling their country to foreigners, to continue being *malinchistas*. Clearly, this represents the creation of reality in its highest form. The play is critical of foreigners whose main goal is to take from Mexico without giving back, and of the *malinchistas* within Mexico. Its message is that Mexico's current reality has been created from without, by the *gringo*, and by Mexicans who continue to sell their own country.

This play, like the rest of López's work and like all of Villegas's, offers little hope for society. López's work is more straightforward, realistic, and theatrically self-conscious than Villegas's, but the message remains the same: there are too many victimizers/dramatists and, more importantly, there are too many willing victims/actors. Seen in this light, the plays of both men express ideas relevant to a broad range of audiences, not just those in Mexico. That is part of the reason these two playwrights achieved the recognition they did. In another sense it was a well-deserved recognition, because the direction they took early in the generation turned out to be the direction followed by the dramatists who came later. Villegas's fragmented style, his language play, and the poetic element in his plays appeared more and more frequently in later works by other dramatists, and López's interest in Mexican history and culture became pervasive, influencing even the novel.[5] This is not to say that either Villegas or López had any direct influence on later writers. The members of this generation had relatively little contact among themselves. The real achievement of the first two writers in the new movement was to anticipate what was to come and what would begin to turn Mexican theater around years later. For this they clearly deserve recognition.

3. The Generation Gap
The First Wave

Like Oscar Villegas and Willebaldo López, many of the dramatists who appeared in the late 1960s began writing in university classes and workshops held by Emilio Carballido. This
was the first large and cohesive group of new writers since the
1950s. However, all of the playwrights, including Villegas and
López, were greeted with such disinterest and even scorn from
public and critics that they stopped writing after only a few
years, and eventually the entire group turned to other endeavors. Some of them managed to publish or stage a few works,
mostly in small magazines, newspaper supplements, or university publications, and on university stages with casts made up
of their peers. Some wrote as many as a dozen plays, but they
were generally short, one-act works; most managed less than
half a dozen plays. This chapter focuses on the earliest attempts
at play production by this group and provides a brief glimpse
of what they wrote later, when some of the dramatists began to
follow directions already explored by Villegas and López.

This new generation of playwrights began with a foundation
of common factors that combined to influence their work. Three
of those factors deserve a few brief comments. First, of course,
is the situation in which they learned—principally with Carballido. Since most of their early works were projects for classes,
they were of necessity short, often one-act sketches. Even the
full-length plays are structured in only two acts or in a series of
brief scenes, such as the strings of fragments that make up Vil-

legas's work. The three-act form that was previously so common disappeared entirely and has yet to reappear.

The second influencing factor is the age of these writers: all were born between 1941 and 1954, which corresponds roughly to the "baby boom" in the United States—the "generation gap" group. This gap existed in Mexico as well, and it became a central focus in a significant percentage of the plays. As a result almost every writer produced at least one play that chronicles the suffering of misunderstood youth brought on by parents, teachers, and society in general, as represented by the older generation, politicians, and the political process.

The third factor, related to the second, is Tlatelolco and the international tensions of 1968. Although those events never became the central topic of any play, they were clearly present in each writer's mind and left their impressions on many of the works produced.[1] In general these playwrights used realistic language, settings, and situations in their presentations of the perceived problems of the younger generation, or of social problems seen from that group's point of view. In many cases the generation gap itself comprises the central thematic material.

Based on these common factors, it is possible to describe four structural and thematic elements that help to define the work of this group of writers. First, their works generally depict a contemporary problem in realistic terms. Second, in many cases the determining factor in the presentation of that reality is the age of the protagonists—teenagers looking from their side of the generation gap. This view of reality creates a division between the characters, but the division has a much broader societal basis—the third element. Whether because of *machismo*, materialism, misunderstanding, selfishness, or perceptions of class structure, positive human relations become almost impossible to achieve. One of the most striking features of most of these plays is the lack of love and the suggestion that close, loving relationships cannot exist. Finally, the most basic theme, and one that can be seen in virtually all of the plays, is that of control: the desire to control one's own life as well as those of others, and the reality of being controlled by others or by circumstances. No characters seem to have control of their situations; there is always someone or something else determining how they must live.

These common aspects—the representation of a contemporary reality, the point of view from the younger side of the generation gap, the lack of strong relationships between people, and the lack of control over one's own circumstance—give a certain unity to this group of works. To some extent, though, that unity appears almost confining, as if each writer felt an obligation to write at least one play dealing with the same problems that concerned his or her peers. This is especially true with the theme of the generation gap. It may be that such insistence contributed to the way the public received this group of writers. The middle class adults who form the majority of the theatergoing public might be somewhat put off by play after play depicting them as driving both the country and its youth to destruction. Whether due to a growing awareness of that situation or to the natural tendency to evolve, the dramatists soon began looking to other areas in search of new themes and new ways to present them.

Eleven playwrights are described in this chapter. Pilar Campesino took possibly the most extreme stance of any of the writers in that her plays deal most directly with violence and revolution. José Agustín, the best known writer in the group, received the most critical attention, primarily on the basis of two works. Dante del Castillo and Miguel Angel Tenorio represent the approaches of the older and younger writers of the generation. The works of other writers—Sergio Peregrina, Jesús Assaf, Felipe Reyes Palacios, Leticia Téllez, Enrique Ballesté, José Luna, and Juan Tovar (most of whom have only one or two plays in print)—provide a view of the range of themes and forms undertaken by this first wave of the new generation.

Pilar Campesino

Pilar Campesino was one of the most strident dramatists of the generation. Her characters seem to embody the hatred and violence of 1968. In *Verano negro* and *Octubre terminó hace mucho tiempo* they are, or perceive themselves to be, revolutionaries, living in a bitter world without humor, happiness, or love.

Verano negro addresses racism and apparently was written in response to the race riots in the United States that summer. Except for one *mestizo* all of the characters are either black or white, and there are both black and white choruses. The play tries to express poetically the hatred of that summer, and the dramatic conflict falls into the same black and white pattern as the characters: the evil whites are condemned for their treatment of the blacks.

A similar potential for violence exists in *Octubre terminó hace mucho tiempo*, but on a more rhetorical level. The play is a dialogue about politics and the need for revolution between two young lovers who consider themselves revolutionaries. Some of their conversation stems from their participation in what seems to be a loosely organized student protest group and from the boy's articles about student violence, one of which in dramatic time foreshadows Tlatelolco: "El Consejo Nacional de Huelga convoca a un mitin y manifestación en la histórica Plaza de las Tres Culturas, el día 2 de octubre, a las 17 horas" (224). This quote represents one of the most direct references to those events in any of the plays.

The pair also touches on the subject of drugs, which leads to scenes in which they take on other identities, read from a novel one of those identities has written, include bits and pieces of English, and condemn their parents. The concerns they express pit them against society as well as against their parents. The result is a constant confrontation between them and the world in which these two seem doomed to suffer alone. The alternate identities add spark to the play and keep it from becoming a lament about long-suffering youth. The play is a representation of present-day reality in which the two characters lack any real control over their lives, although control seems to be one of their principal desires. In addition, real love and even a positive relationship are missing from their lives. Campesino's play differs from many other works with similar themes in that it is more infused with a hatred that threatens to explode into serious violence. *Octubre* also resembles, perhaps more than any other Mexican play of this generation, the strongly sociopolitical drama of other Latin American countries.

Campesino did not write again until 1979, the same year that marks the beginning of the second wave of writers. The new play, *Superocho*, shows a new focus and a new theme. The action no longer centers on the confrontation between teenagers and their parents and the system; the question of control is now associated with the doubtful status of reality. The origin of reality becomes the central focus in the decade of the eighties, and *Superocho* is a good example of that concern. The question of what is real presents itself first in the title, which appears variously as *Superocho, Ese ocho, S 8, Ese 8* (all on the title page in *Tramoya*), and *eSe 8* (in the bibliographic information of *Más teatro joven*, p. 242). There is no apparent reason for the different spellings; the effect is to make any written reference to the play confusing—a reflection of the confusion the characters experience. Revolution and violence continue as Campesino's primary themes, but this time in the context of a film being produced by the characters. The distinction between reality and film begins to blur for Rodrigo, the film's director, as seen in the following conversation between him and Cecilia, his wife, who is also the author of the screenplay:

> RODRIGO: (*de pronto*): Aclárame una cosa, mi vida: ¿Cecilia le está escribiendo a Rodrigo qué, una obra de teatro, una película, las dos cosas, una obra de teatro sobre la filmación de una película o un argumento cinematográfico sobre una obra de teatro?
> CECILIA: Eso justamente quisiera yo que tú me aclararas.
> RODRIGO: Necesito saber cuántos planos estás manejando, ¿me explico? Uno, el de Cecilia, es decir tú como autora, totalmente independiente del enjuague; dos, el de Cecilia, es decir tú como personaje creado por Cecilia autora, que es también escritora y autora a la vez de la pieza, argumento, guión, drama o como quieras llamarlo; tres, el de Cecilia esposa de Rodrigo cineasta; cuatro . . . (*El silencio de ella lo obliga a reflexionar.*) ¿Está muy jalado de los pelos?
> CECILIA: (*confundida*): No tengo la menor idea, corazón. Lo único que sé con toda certeza es que llevo meses tratando de encontrarle una razón a lo que estoy escribiendo. (*Tramoya 20*, 81)

This kind of runaway reality and the desire to create reality for others, a sort of play in which they will have to act, was one of the most important concerns of the young dramatists in the 1980s. The change in Campesino's focus between her first two plays and her third is significant because her shift from a predominantly political theme to one that questions the composition of reality suggests the kind of change that became common with later playwrights.

José Agustín

If Campesino's production was sporadic, José Agustín's was even more so. In fact, he published only three plays, two of which achieved a degree of fame or perhaps notoriety. The themes, characters, and language of his novels of *la onda* also appear in his plays, which focus on young people and their problems. His two most important plays were written during the first wave of the generation.

Abolición de la propiedad is a conversation between two young people. According to Bruce-Novoa, "The plot is the confrontation of two fundamentally opposite types: Norma, the young liberal who believes in love, justice, revolution, personal freedom, nonconformity, etc.; and Everio, a young conservative who believes in conforming to society, the validity of national traditions and the established moral absolutes" (6). The fact that a study of this play has been published is significant, since less than half a dozen plays of the entire generation received any critical attention outside of a few articles in Mexican newspaper supplements. Part of the interest in *Abolición de la propiedad* derives from its staging requirements: aside from the basic set (a basement room) the play requires tape recorders, slides, film, projectors, television monitors, and a live rock band. One of the fundamental themes concerns the idea of control, as Norma herself indicates: "En realidad si encuentro a alguien más tímido que yo automáticamente me siento segura. También me pasa al revés" (19). George Woodyard described the play as "a constant jockeying for position—to dominate or be dominated" (32). The struggle is not just between the two characters, though; some other power is also involved.

While waiting for a friend to return, Norma turns on a tape recorder that happens to be in the room. Much to her surprise she hears a conversation between herself and a boy. Everio, also a friend of the friend, enters and before long Norma finds that she and Everio are repeating the conversation she heard earlier. This happens throughout the play. Every time Everio makes one of his frequent trips to the bathroom, she turns on the tape recorder, hears another fragment of conversation, and after he returns they eventually repeat it. The theme of control enters here at its most fundamental level. While Norma and Everio appear to feel some attraction for each other, the development of the relationship is continually stymied by outside factors that conspire against them. The tape recording preoccupies Norma and eventually leads Everio to attack her physically. In addition, Norma is unable to keep her contact lens in place, and the effect of Everio's nerves on his bladder repeatedly interrupts their conversation. These little annoyances indicate the lack of control that is suggested by all the gadgetry—the technology that dominates and encroaches on their, and most people's, lives. Because technology affects both old and young, the control theme is not portrayed as a "generation gap" problem.

However, *Abolición* still exhibits the four characteristics of most of this generation's work. The *onda* dialogue and the music situate the action in a present-time reality; the lack of control leads to the breakdown in the relationship that seems to be beginning, so that love or even friendship becomes impossible. The focus on teenagers, although it is not dominant, is also typical of the first wave of this generation.

Círculo vicioso fits this pattern as well. The action centers on four boys who find themselves in Lecumberri prison after being arrested and charged with the intent to sell drugs. The situation provides the opportunity to show a society that is corrupt and out of control, but that still maintains the pretense of control. Since the prison is essentially run by the prisoners, some of whom benefit financially from their control, the boys find themselves with no faith in the "real" officials and doubts about who to trust in the next level of "unofficials." Another prisoner warns them to keep a wary eye on the *mayor* and the *licenciado*, the two who run that section of the prison: "Yo no dije eso, qué pasó. Nomás dije que lo pensaran bien. El mayor y el licenciado andan tras los quintos, como todos, y son expertos en el arte del verbo" (51). Apparently no one can be trusted, especially those who exercise direct control over the situation. The boys, however, are not innocent victims who provide a contrast with the corruption that surrounds them. Instead they reflect the closed society in which they are trapped. One minute they swear to the *mayor* that they have no money to pay for the rent on their cell or for hot food or other amenities, and the next they dig into their pockets for money to buy marijuana from one of the prisoners.

All of the characters possess one common trait: they are concerned solely with themselves and their own welfare. This "look-out-for-number-one" mentality develops in great part as a result of the pervading corruption and greed that surrounds them. The play's criticism of these attitudes and conditions clearly applies to all of society, not just to the prison. When they are warned that the key to their survival is money, one of the boys replies, "También afuera. Afuera es igual que aquí, nada más que con coches" (49).

While the young do suffer in this play, the fault is clearly their own. The indictment of society is still there, however, since it provides the atmosphere that encourages and even rewards corrupt behavior. The play depicts a reality in which greed and corruption are so entrenched that no one can trust anyone else and no one can really exercise control. These two concerns may be the real message behind all the suffering teens in so many of the generation's early plays, but Agustín was the first to suggest that not just parents but all of society is responsible for the current circumstances.

The attention that *Círculo vicioso* attracted when first produced was more governmental than critical. Supposedly because of the obscene language there was an attempt to censor the play. It is one of the more overt attempts at censorship, although it does not approach the degree exercised by some of the more restrictive governments in Latin America.

Dante del Castillo

Dante del Castillo also extends his criticism to all of society. Among the writers of the first wave, he was one of those who moved most quickly to diversify thematic material and style. He did, however, write one play—*Riesgo, vidrio*—that criticizes parents, specifically the father. The tension is created by the father's attitude toward his family. At one point the wife objects: "Yo soy *tu* esposa y ellos son *tus* hijos, pero ni ellos ni yo somos objetos que puedas tratar como se te antoje . . . Hace un rato te decía que tratas a los muchachos como a unos niños, pero no era la palabra correcta, los tratas como máquinas para manejar a tu antojo" (257). The father attempts to control his children to rectify his own failure. He wants them, and especially the oldest boy, to have what he never had—mainly the opportunity to study business, which the boy does not want. Unlike the case in other, similar plays, this boy's rebellion ends with a satisfactory resolution, but the play still contains three of the four basic characteristics: realism, the themes of control, and the generation gap. However, Castillo soon employed other situations to express his themes.

El gerente focuses on lack of control and selfishness in the context of a manager who tries to suppress his company's guilt in the death of a worker. The manager and indeed nearly all the characters devote themselves to hiding their own involvement and manipulating the situation to their advantage. As in *Círculo vicioso*, money and selfishness lead to separation instead of unity and eliminate the chances for positive relationships. These are characteristics that all of the young dramatists criticized, but Castillo did so from the perspective of adults instead of teenagers. He even managed a subtle criticism of the United States, since the manager's name is "Kódac."

Four years after *El gerente*, Castillo explored other themes in *Adán, Eva y la otra*, which offers an explanation for the Oedipus complex. In this play, a happily married man is seduced by Death, in the form of a beautiful woman. As soon as he is won over, he begins to regret his actions, primarily because the mysterious *Señora* will not be devoting all of her time to him any longer. He finally decides to work out a deal whereby he can return to his wife, although now as her baby and with a father whom he already dislikes. *Adán, Eva y la otra*, with death incarnate on stage, is less realistic than Castillo's previous plays. His move away from teenage characters indicates not only maturity, but also a search for more universal themes, or at least a broader base for the theme of control. Like the manager in *El gerente* and the father in *Riesgo, vidrio, Adán* is characterized by the desire for personal gratification and control, which once again makes love cheap or impossible.

Six years later some of the dramatic elements in *Adán, Eva y la otra* reappeared in *Mulata con magia y plata*. Here, the title character is credited with winning freedom for black slaves during the Colonial period in the New World. She is aided by gods who create rain and wind, bring one character back from the dead, and perform other miraculous acts that save the Mulata from the Inquisition and allow her to cause the Viceroy to give freedom and land to the blacks. The play's social message is mitigated somewhat by the songs and dances—Castillo calls the work a "Comedia musical en dos actos." Its characters, unlike those in earlier works, do find love, so the play ends on a positive note. By the time he wrote *Mulata con magia y plata*, Castillo had begun to look to history for dramatic material and had completely changed his perspective to that of adults.

Miguel Angel Tenorio

Unlike Castillo, Miguel Angel Tenorio found new ways to express his social concerns and still maintain teenagers as his focus. His *En español se dice abismo* provides an example of the kind of play that was common during the early years of the generation.

The title refers to the widening of the generation gap to become an *abismo*. The first act is an emotional confrontation between a daughter and her parents after she comes home late one night. Although she attempts to evade her parents' questions, it is eventually learned that she has spent the evening with a boy the parents do not consider suitable. The girl likes him because he is different—a rebel, as she considers herself to be. Her parents are depicted as unreasonable, making no attempt to understand her, and continuing to insist that the boy is beneath her. Ironically, in the transition scene between the first and second acts, it is learned that the father has a mistress on the side.

Later, when the girl suspects she may be pregnant, the boy's shallow *machismo* is revealed, as he wishes to end the relationship and even offers a bribe to do so. However, when the girl's parents demand a marriage, it is she who refuses and runs away. The suggestion is that the girl, and therefore most teenagers, know more about what is best for them than do their parents.

All of the standard elements are represented here. The play presents a contemporary reality in the language, characterization, and theme. Everyone wants to control the young people, no one does, and all that is created is a separation, the *abismo*. Any hopes for control, love, and positive relationships are cancelled by hypocrisy, stubborness, selfishness, and *machismo*. Obviously there is a gap, and it exists between more than just generations.

Tenorio's social and political concerns formed the core of his other 1975 play, *Cambio de valencia o el espíritu de la lucha*. The first act shows Marx and Engels as they work on the *Communist Manifesto*, and the second act shows what their ideas have become today. They do not begin with a very solid base, since in Act I Marx has moved in with Engels, is eating his food, and in half an hour finishes off a bottle of wine that was supposed to last several days. In Act II Marx and Engels return as Carlos and Federico and attend a political meeting dominated by devotees of Mao and Che Guevara. The message is that today's communist rebels (at least those in Mexico) have lost sight of pure communism. The meeting deteriorates into a shouting match and then into anarchy as each group insists on its own views. As the demagoguery increases, it becomes obvious that this group will never initiate a unified revolution. Marx declares, "Yo, Carlos Marx, en pleno uso de mis facultades mentales y en vista de las circunstancias, declaro no saber nada acerca del comunismo," and Engels seconds the sentiments (247). The solution that suggests itself is a return to basics, but that possibility is doubtful also, since Marx has already been portrayed as a freeloader and an alcoholic in the first act.

Whatever the view of these fictionalized Communists, the

play makes a familiar comment on the real world: nobody is in control because there is no unity, only a selfish interest in gaining control. By 1978, though, Tenorio had somewhat modified this pessimistic view.

El día que Javier se puso águila returns to the theme of uncaring parents and confused youth, but now with the historical element that became an important concern in the 1980s. In this play, Javier must write a composition for school. He does not complete it before bedtime, and it reappears in a dream that turns into a history lesson. A serpent representing darkness and figures that depict hunger and ignorance are seen as they repeatedly try to take power in Mexico. These evil characters are opposed by the "Eagle" and a series of Mexican heroes (such as Hidalgo and Juárez), along with several youngsters who represent the Mexican people. The defenders of good always win, but ignorance invariably escapes and comes back to cause more problems. At the end it is still not clear whether ignorance has been defeated or whether the people will allow it to appear again.

Like so many of his fellow dramatists, Tenorio turned to a broader Mexican reality—its history and its culture—as he continued to write. It was still a Mexican reality, where the lack of control and the immense separations between young and old, men and women, social classes, and political groups do not allow unity and smother any hope for love. Beneath everything is the suggestion that the younger generation suffers now and may continue to suffer because of the stupidity of the older generation.

Sergio Peregrina

Sergio Peregrina took this same suggestion, exaggerated it into farce, and defined it in terms of a struggle between civilization and nature, human and animal urges, reason and instinct. According to Peregrina, instinct always wins. Peregrina produced only a few very short sketches, then stopped writing. His works are notable for their humor, which he used more than other dramatists of the time, and the way he defines the theme of control.

In an unpublished skit called *Dúo de cuatro*, a woman with her cat and a man with his dog meet in a park. Apparently they live together, or at least have a close relationship. She defines their association early in the play: "Lo que pasa es que todo el tiempo estamos como perros y gatos." This turns out to be a literal description because, as the two fight, make up, fight, and make up, the dog and the cat begin to participate in the dialogue. They simply speak lines that their owners could have spoken. After the initial surprise caused by talking dogs and cats on stage, the fact that animals and people are interchangeable does not seem at all unusual since the animals are at least as rational as the humans. In fact, when the humans plan to separate at the end, the cat saves the relationship by speaking the last line of the play: "¡No te vayas, ven. Ven mañana al parque, ven!" Having the cat take the initiative suggests that at times a basic animal instinct takes control of people's actions, which may have some bearing on the survival-of-the-fittest mentality that appears in so many of the plays already discussed.

In *Cocina vegetariana* the human and animal levels fuse. A salesman who sells vegetarian cookbooks door-to-door arrives at the apartment of a lady who favors cannibalism. She spends her time trying to seduce the nervous salesman, and finally entices him into sitting with her on the sofa. As the lights fade, she yells at her "children" (who make their own animal-like sounds), "Cállense malditos, no puede una ni comer a gusto" (67). This concern with self at the most basic level is not much removed from some of the behavior of various supposedly civilized characters in other plays of the generation. Peregrina merely defines it in its starkest terms.

Volver a decir el mar, which appears in *Teatro joven de México*, follows the popular line of the two suffering teenagers. He is unemployed and unenthusiastic, she is pregnant, neither has parental support, love, or control over their situation; they are running away to a marriage that neither wants. The boy laments their situation while waiting for the girl, who is in a confessional. This is one of only a few monologues written in the first wave.

Young Love and Control: *Teatro joven de México*

The first *Teatro joven de México* contained several plays by writers who did not continue a steady production thereafter. Three works center on the trials of young love, and three others look at how reality might be controlled.

In Jesús Assaf's *Estoy enamorado de tu hermana*, a boy attempts to work out his feelings for two sisters, frequently narrating the situation in asides to the audience. He loves one and befriends the other. The latter tries to break them apart because she loves the boy. In the end, true love triumphs, and the "bad" sister learns her lesson and leaves home so as not to interfere with the relationship.

Felipe Reyes Palacios also presented two young lovers who have to struggle against the girl's sister. Additionally the boy feels the need to struggle against parents and society, as he explains in his relatively frequent asides to the audience. The play ends inconclusively with the hint that an unwanted pregnancy will further complicate the situation.

Leticia Téllez, one of only a few female dramatists, offered a woman's viewpoint of the trials of love. The female student in *La tercera ley de Newton* initially rejects the advances of a fellow student because she is involved with their professor. When the professor admits that he is married, she stops loving him and, almost as an act of vengeance or desperation, agrees to go out with the boy after all.

In Enrique Ballesté's *Mínimo quiere saber*, the title character essentially fakes his way into a police uniform and is given the assignment of watching over a playground for gifted students. The snobbish students do not want their area contaminated by any ungifted persons so, when he will not leave on his own, they finally convince Mínimo to commit suicide. The play deals with idealism, lost innocence, and the question of God's existence. The action is substantially different from that of most of the other plays, but thematically the focus still falls on the idea of control—who has it, who lacks it, and how one attains it.

With *El hacha* José Luna anticipated Peregrina's civilization–nature dichotomy. A couple goes on vacation in the woods. He is interested in seeing the sights while she is interested in sex. When he rebuffs her advances, she occupies her time "educating" a backwoodsman, and in the end he returns to the city with her while the husband stays behind to live in nature. In terms of reason and instinct, the play becomes interestingly convo-

luted: which triumphs? Although at times the woman lacks control, she has more than either of the men. She is driven by
instinct, but she achieves her desire through reason (teaching),
and returns to civilization at the end. Like so many of this generation's plays, there is no real love involved; relationships are
still based on self-centered motives.

In many ways the work of Juan Tovar is atypical of his generation. He adapted prose works, collaborated with other writers, and used historical settings for his drama. In *Markheim*,
adapted from a story by Robert Louis Stevenson, a man murders
a shop owner, then is presented with the chance to continue a
life of crime or to reform. He chooses the latter, thereby suggesting a degree of control not seen in the works of Tovar's
contemporaries. It may be significant that the action came from
the ideas of a non-Mexican.

This first group of plays shows a picture of Mexico in the last
years of the 1960s, seen through the eyes of the younger generation. They painted that picture on the foundation of a contemporary Mexican reality, the real world depicted realistically
on stage. The characters, many times teenagers, find themselves
alone, separated from their parents, their teachers, and the rest
of the older generation and society, and separated from each
other because they seem unable to feel real love or experience
true concern for others. Instead they find themselves trapped
in the same game as their elders: the struggle to escape from
the control of others and to establish control not only over their
own lives, but over the lives of those around them. Unfortunately
it is a struggle that always seems to result in failure.

4. A Five-Year Lull, 1974-1978
Velásquez

The year 1973 should have been the turning point for Mexican theater's new generation. A fresh, new group of young writers had just had a selection of their plays published, Emilio Carballido and Luisa Josefina Hernández figured among their teachers and supporters, and many of the important dramatists who had formed the theater vanguard for the preceding twenty years had reduced their production or ceased writing altogether. However, a simple glance at any *cartelera teatral* of the period suggests why the new dramatists failed to find support from the public. Foreign plays (including American musicals such as *My Fair Lady*) and tacky "bedroom comedies" dominated the offerings. At that point Mexican was "out," foreign was "in," and the public seemed more interested in escapism and light entertainment than in social commentary. As a result the anthology put together by Carballido quickly disappeared, as did most of the playwrights. High on their list of reasons were frustration and economics. The theater establishment—theaters and publishers—ignored and even criticized the new writers, and when it became impossible for them to earn a living in the theater, they turned to other activities. Some of them wrote another play or two, but thirteen of the fifteen writers included in that first *Teatro joven de México* effectively stopped trying, at least for a time. The first wave of writers in the generation simply ceased to exist as playwrights. The next five years, until the publication of the second *Teatro joven de México,* became a time for regrouping and an opportunity for the members who formed the second wave to learn and gather momentum.

It is worth noting a coincidence between the division of new Mexican theater into three periods and the nearly identical demarkation proposed for new Puerto Rican drama by Roberto Ramos-Perea. He defines two cycles of growth, the first beginning in 1968 and ending in 1975, the second extending from 1978 to 1986 (62). These years correspond well to the time frame of Mexico's first and second waves of dramatists (1967 to 1973, and 1979 to 1985). The importance of 1968 as a seminal year in Latin American theater is also supported by Leonardo Azparren Giménez's designation of that year as the beginning of a new generation of Venezuelan dramatists. The designation of a transition period in Puerto Rico (1976–1978) also lends credence to the idea of a similar period of regrouping in Mexico. Ramos-Perea speaks of an "abismo generacional" and a "crisis de dramaturgos" (61) in Puerto Rico. The exclusion of these writers from the mainstream, so similar to what happened in Mexico, may well sap the energy from a generation or movement and force its members to step back and reevaluate their work. That was certainly the case in Mexico.

Among the thirty-nine works written by members of the new generation between 1974 and 1978, no less than ten were written by Gerardo Velásquez. Hector Berthier and Reynaldo Carballido added nine more. These three playwrights are featured in detail in this chapter. Other members of the generation combined for thirteen of the remaining twenty plays.[1] Willebaldo López contributed two plays before becoming involved in other theater projects. Miguel Angel Tenorio completed six plays and then began to write for television. Dante del Castillo finished three plays during this period, and Jesús González Dávila (see chapter 5) contributed two children's plays.

Reynaldo Carballido

Although Reynaldo Carballido began to write in 1973, his plays are very much a throwback to those of the first wave; he simply started writing later than those dramatists. His early works featured the same themes and have the same feel as plays in the first wave. A shift in the point of view of two more recent plays, though, added new depth to his thematic expression. The picture he painted of Mexico City in the 1960s and 1970s is highly critical and does not present a very pleasant scene. Seemingly 99 percent of the school-age boys were primarily interested in sex, drinking, and being *macho*, and they learned corruption from the police, the bureaucrats, and their teachers (who were also interested in sex—with the students). Truly loving relationships were nonexistent. The governmental bureaucracy is depicted as a mass of red tape, favoritism, nepotism, corruption, and inefficiency. Some of the plays bear a resemblance to the sketches on the popular Mexican television program, "¿Qué nos pasa?" albeit without the humor. The plays collected under the title *Los mandamientos de la ley del hombre* illustrate the various ways he presented his criticism.

In *Moto en delegación* a boy tries to discover who stole several parts from his motorcycle while it was in the custody of the officials after an accident. Everyone in the office covers for everyone else, the bosses chase the secretaries, and for some reason the person responsible for the thefts strangles a secretary, at which point everyone feels free to reveal that he was responsible not only for this theft, but for many others. In *La señora de gris*, a twenty- year- old boy looks for ways to convince a lonely older woman that it is all right for the two of them to go to the movie together. His none-too-subtle reasons are really directed at convincing her to go to bed with him. The girl in *El periódico* is younger than the boy, and neither is as self-assured as the characters in *La señora de gris*, but they are involved in the same process—the search for a justification that will allow them to have sex without feeling guilty. *Acto social* continues basically the same theme, but now in a homosexual relationship. The last play, which bears the same title as the collection, changes direction and features young people against the system. A group of students stages an uprising because of the arcane rules insisted upon by school authorities. The plays are didactic, showing why the bureaucracy is bad and why sex is natural.

La corriente, written in 1978, takes a decidedly more social approach. It begins as a group of boys, with the acquiescence of a policeman, tries to rape three American girls. One of the boys helps one of the girls to escape but then turns on her, although he finally stops, partly because they are lost and partly because they are at the scene of a demonstration that turns violent. The same characteristics appear again—boys interested in sex, drinking, and being *macho*; violence encouraged by a corrupt police; and a litany of complaints about society and government. To an extent, the play can be considered sociology as much as drama because one of its primary goals is the depiction of society at the time.

The focus is narrower, but the same strong criticism is present, in *Sombras ajenas* (1980). In this case abusive professors are the target, and the example is one who is having an affair with a student who dies, apparently after an abortion. This information is revealed in a confrontation between the teacher and another student with whom he is involved. The message is that professors, like all authority figures, take advantage of those beneath them and the end result is pain and suffering.

Two of Carballido's more recent plays, *Nosotros, los de entonces* and *Cuestión de prácticas*, maintained the social focus, but a new perspective gave them additional depth. In the first play El and Ella meet after a ten-year separation. Both of them have lost their youthful, rebellious idealism. He has become one of the bureaucrats he protested against previously; she has allowed herself to be kept by a man who disgusts her. She has decided, however, to return to her village and begin life anew. Her afternoon love-making with the man serves that purpose: she hopes to become pregnant, leave the man, have her child, and work to make a contribution to her hometown.

Cuestión de prácticas begins with a typical students' point of view, but with an added touch of humor that enhances the social criticism. The principal characters are several young ladies about to embark on the "real-life," field-work portion of their education as social workers. This unlikely group of candidates is totally unprepared, both educationally and socially, for what awaits them. They complain about the bad odors, are unsure if they are in a *colonia* or a *municipio* (27) and what the difference is, and they are completely ignorant about what they are supposed to do there. They encounter various unsavory types whose very unsavoriness makes the students' naive idealism seem less objectionable. Eventually one of the would-be social workers finds herself forced into the position of spokesperson for the *barrio* women who demand gas, electric, water, and sewage services but refuse to pay the fees the politicians claim must be collected. The hypocritical government representatives resolve the confrontation with violence, thus taking on the role of villains and elevating the still naive but now involved students another rung on the ladder of acceptability. Ironically, those least prepared to do good find themselves working to improve housing conditions, while the officials who are responsible for maintaining decent living standards do nothing and even make matters worse. This irony and the students' unwitting rise to social commitment maintain tension in the play and make its social message more effective.

Although Carballido's plays have movement and action, dialogue predominates, since that is the vehicle through which the message is communicated. The characters also tend to serve that purpose; more than fulfilling a dramatic function, they exist to convey the plays' central message or lesson. As a result, Carballido's plays are, to a great extent, sociological studies that serve to paint a depressing and pessimistic picture of Mexico.

Hector Berthier

Hector Berthier began to write during the five-year lull, and although his production has been minimal to date, his works merit comment, in part because of their wide range. His first play (*Romeo y Julieta, Acto Tercero, Escena Quinta*) is the "obligatory" one-act describing the rough course of young love, while his last is a fantasy set in a past time, a far-away land, and featuring Aladdin and his magic lamp (*Cuentan, entre las cosas que cuentan*). Here it is suggested that rampant materialism seemingly reaps rewards. Berthier's most interesting play, though, is *El Corsario Negro*, a multi-layered work that sets side-by-side a big city–small town oppositon and a Mexico–United States comparison.

In a small-town bus station (the play takes its title from the name of the bus line), Manuel waits for a late-night bus to Mexico

City, where he is returning after a short and not very enjoyable visit with a distant relative who lives in the town. As he waits he talks with the ticket agent, and their conversation expresses the commonly held idea that the city is better than a town because the former offers more opportunities, more money, and in general a better life. Later the agent leaves for a time, and Manuel begins to talk with another passenger, Cintia, who lives in the town and whose mother is Mexican and whose father is North American. With the boy's preference for the city already determined, their conversation turns to a comparison between the Mexican capital and the United States in general, and she insists that the latter is preferable. Thus the play establishes a hierarchy in which small-town Mexico occupies the bottom rung, any place in the United States the top, and Mexico City the middle. The decision of these two young people to leave the town is, therefore, credible.

However, Cintia, the representative of the United States, soon demonstrates a contrasting side. She may be attractive on the outside, but the more she talks, the more she shows herself to be egotistical, demanding, and condescending. When the bus finally arrives she leaves, but Manuel decides to stay behind. His decision is based on an inversion of the previously established hierarchy, and the audience is left with the feeling that small-town life is not so horrible after all. Its simplicity may be preferable to life in the big city, and certainly to that in the United States.

This play is interesting because it engages a wider range of social issues than most of the plays that appeared before, it takes place in a different setting, the characters are fuller, and the criticism of life in Mexico City is subtler. Some moments in the play could almost be considered simple *cuadros de costumbre*, but this play (and to some extent *Cuentan, entre las cosas que cuentan*) also fits into the larger pattern of myth described by Joseph Campbell in *The Hero with a Thousand Faces*. This adds a depth to its structure not present in many of the other plays written during the earlier period.

Campbell's myth structure defines three stages, each with several subsections.

Departure	Initiation	Return
The Call to Adventure	The Road of Trials	Refusal of the Return
	The Meeting with	
Refusal of the Call	the Goddess	The Magic Flight
Supernatural Aid	Woman as Temptress	Rescue from Without
The Crossing of the	Atonement with	The Crossing of the
First Threshold	the Father	Return Threshold
The Belly of		
the Whale	Apotheosis	Master of Two Worlds
	The Ultimate Boon	Freedom to Live

All five steps of the first stage can be found in *El Corsario* Negro. The first two occur before the staged action, when Manuel travel to visit his father's relative, despite his preference for a vacation elsewhere. The next three are present in the first part of the play, although somewhat out of order. Manuel enters the bus station ("Crossing of the First Threshold"), it is night ("Belly of the Whale"), and the ticket agent talks him into playing a game of chance while they wait, a game that Manuel does not know but that he proceeds to win nonetheless ("Supernatural Aid"?). Campbell's second stage, "Trials and Victories of Initiation," has six substages. The ones that appear most clearly in this play are "The Road of Trials," "The Meeting with the Goddess," and "Woman as the Temptress," when Cintia arrives and preaches the superiority of the United States. Less obvious are "Atonement with the Father," "Apotheosis," and "The Ultimate Boon," when Manuel realizes that his disdain for the town was inappropriate. This leads to the final stage, "Return and Reintegration with Society" and three of its substages, during which Manuel not only decides to stay in the town, but goes behind the desk to watch the bus station while the regular agent is away trying to patch up a fight he had with his wife—"Crossing of the Return Threshold," "Master of Two Worlds," and "Freedom to Live."

The presence of such a structure suggests a more important lesson learned than simply that adults, government, and society are bad things. This extra level adds depth to the characters, interest to the play, and helps to make it Berthier's most accomplished work. It is coincidental but somehow appropriate that it should appear in the second of the three stages followed by Mexico's young generation of dramatists. Having set out on their own in the first wave ("Separation and Departure") and been rejected, the generation found itself at a crossroads: will a whole generation founder and disappear, or will it survive ("Trials and Victories of Initiation")? As it happened, the road to the "Return and Reintegration with Society" was paved, at least in some sense, by Gerardo Velásquez, whose works embody many of the elements that became important when the second wave of dramatists began to write.

Gerardo Velásquez

Velásquez represents almost a complete break with the themes, characters, and settings of the generation's first wave of playwrights, and his work forecast the direction and the concerns that occupied later dramatists. His work can be divided into two parts: one group of "small town" plays and another of historical plays. Both groups have in common a fragmented structure that forces the reader or spectator to arrange the pieces in a kind of puzzle, and that demands a conscious involvement in the development of the action.

Velásquez's first works date from 1973 and 1974 and include seven one-act plays collected in *Tramoya 4* under the title *Amapolas*, as well as two longer plays written in 1976 and 1977. Like the playwrights before him, Velásquez concerned himself with the difficulty of maintaining relationships, but his point of view was not that of the young, and his characters were not teenagers. He was concerned with people on a wider scale and many times he focused on women, allowing the female characters to establish the tone. His setting was the countryside, not Mexico City, and his themes were incorporated into his stories. The stories do not exist merely to communicate the themes.

Women and structural presentation occupy a prominent place in Velásquez's drama. Women are particularly important in the early works. If they are not the protagonists, they are still central to the themes, and all of them are alone, lonely, abused, or misused, in one combination or another. Yet the plays do not present overt lamentations of these situations. Rather, the problems and difficulties are woven into stories dealing with, among other topics, incest, robbery, adultery, and lesbianism.

Structure also plays a central part in the unfolding of the themes because it forces the participation of the reader or spectator. In the short plays collected under the title *Amapolas*, all of the stories develop on the basis of a fundamental, five-part sequence. There is always an occurrence previous to the action of the play itself, and therefore unknown to the audience. After a brief opening scene a character enters who will provide information to the audience, or the other characters, or both. At this point readers, spectators, and other characters can begin to try to unravel the mystery arising from that previous action. The mystery eventually becomes clear due to the accumulation of additional information, usually provided by the arrival of one or more new characters. Then, in most cases, there is a departure that signals the end of the action and appears to suggest a resolution, but actually represents the continuation of a spiral—the original situation is modified, but remains essentially the same. Such a structure calls to mind the codes proposed in *S/Z*, Roland Barthes's detailed study of *Sarrasine*. Mentioning them briefly helps to clarify Velásquez's process.

Underlying all the other codes is the *referential* code, a broadly based and somewhat imprecise code that pertains to a body of common cultural knowledge. In most of the plays mentioned in previous chapters, that knowledge involved Mexican society, culture, and government as they existed in Mexico City in the 1960s and early 1970s. In most of Velásquez's work it involved the same elements in a rural setting. Barthes's *proairetic* code, the plot or the sequence of events, unfolds the mystery in Velásquez's plays. The five steps mentioned before are organized under this code. The mystery itself involves the relationships among the characters and thus points to the *semic* or *connotative* code. The *symbolic* code echoes, provides clues to, or rounds out the puzzle and varies in its role from drama to drama. The *hermeneutic* code, the enigmas and questions posed by the text and directed to the characters, the audience, or both, underlies the whole enterprise because it is this code that forces interaction with the events. If the audience or reader chooses to continue to follow the dramatic action, participation becomes essential because the hermeneutic element does not allow for passivity in these plays.

As Velásquez's En "El Gato Negro" opens, one man alone in a bar searches for change for the juke box. A knock at the door interrupts him, and the caller, a llamador, demands "¡Déjame entrar! Su esposa me dijo que estaba aquí" (20). When the man refuses to open, the caller asks, "¿Por qué tanto misterio?" The man answers, "¿Cuál misterio? Aquí no hay misterios. ¿Por qué habría de haberlos?" (20). The hermeneutic code immediately gains prominence if for no other reason than the insistence of the man's denial. When the llamador finally gains entrance, the two men drink and discuss money, women, and wives, and in particular the man's wife. "Rechula que está su vieja. Parece una artista de cine," comments the caller. The man replies, "Soy un cabrón, con mi vieja soy un cabrón. No quiero ser tan ojete con ella" (24). Nevertheless, he soon asks, "Y usted, ¿cuánto me va a dar por ella, compadre?" (24). When the caller asks for a clarification, the man answers, "No me haga caso, yo creo que ya estoy bien borracho," after which the stage directions indicate, "Se entreabre la puerta que está cerca del mostrador. Se oyen risas" (24). At that point the cantinero emerges from the back and sends the caller on his way. It finally becomes clear that the man has rented his wife to the cantinero, a fact confirmed when she too emerges from the back room waving a pistol. All three characters hurl drunken, empty threats at each other until the husband and wife finally leave, putting an end to this episode, but not really resolving the situation or the couple's relationship.

The brief scene before the arrival of the caller establishes the tone and atmosphere (the referential code) in En "El Gato Negro". They are primarily the atmosphere of a Mexican small-town bar, the element of machismo, and to a certain extent the economic conditions in such a place. The proairetic code and the semic code intertwine in the business deal between the man, the bar owner, and the wife, since that relationship provides the movement behind the scenes. The conversation between the man and the caller involves the proairetic and symbolic codes, although the latter is confined more to the play's title. The hermeneutic code unifies all the rest of the codes. The enigma was established in the deal struck prior to the action of the play, the first step in Velásquez's five-part structure. The conversation between the man and the caller forms the foundation of the play since the man's mood and sometimes elusive or out-of-context comments provoke the curiosity of both the caller and the audience. The caller, as much in the dark as the spectators, supplies many of the questions that they would ask were they able. Since he departs before the resolution, he appears to be the only one left with an unresolved mystery. However, his earlier comment ("Su esposa me dijo que estaba aquí") suggests he knows more than one might think. How, when, and even why he got that information from the wife while she was in the back room with the bar owner remains a puzzle and leaves at least one unanswered question.

A second question concerns the relationship between the man and his wife: have they been reconciled, or will the same thing happen again in the future? A primary characteristic of Velásquez's work is his open-endedness. Nothing is as simple as it might seem. These kinds of doubts about what really happens became a fundamental element of the plays that appeared in the second wave.

Unresolvable mysteries play an even greater part in *El cuarto más tranquilo*, which owes much to Juan Rulfo's *Pedro Páramo*. The other plays in the collection follow the same pattern but are increasingly melancholy, focus more on female characters, and stress their condition as lonely, without hope, and almost always lacking in control over the events that affect them.

La huerta deals principally with the question of control. In fact, that seems to be the primary goal of the men in the play. The characters still find themselves basically alone; they have only minimal contact. The structure reflects the stylized, almost poetic dialogue, since the scenes are based on groupings of the three male and three female characters into geometrical forms, each corresponding to an "act"—"Sexteto," a hexagon; "Una estrella a medio hacer," two overlapping triangles (a star); and "Asterisco," an asterisk. The title and the overall feel of the play suggest the Biblical Garden, thus establishing the male-female conflict over who had control at the very beginning of human existence. In the process Velásquez managed to summarize in two lines of dialogue the anguish that most of his predecessors tried to convey by using whole plays. La Muchacha says, "Tengo los pies llagados," and El Muchacho replies, "Primero son los pies, luego el tronco, la cabeza, el alma" (41).

If the structure of *La huerta* is based on geometrical patterns, that of *Toño Basura* revolves around a mathematical and logical puzzle. The play, and indeed Velásquez's work in general, also reflects the play's subtitle: "Retrato cubista." A brief, somewhat superficial catalogue of characteristics describes cubism as a conceptual, intellectual art form that is realistic in an iconographic sense, employing geometric forms. In fact, form itself becomes a part of the communicative process. Form, as a means of expression along with multiple viewpoints, helps to create dynamism, a kind of life and physical movement where one might logically expect a static presentation, in a painting for example. This inner movement, different from dramatic movement or the hermeneutic code, pulls the audience into the experience of Velásquez's plays. Finally, as a school, cubism moved from recognizable to more hermetic works. Velásquez's plays follow a similar pattern of development.[2]

Toño Basura is Velásquez's most concentrated cubist experiment. The play has four parts, each with its own set of metaphors corresponding to a direction, a season, a color, and an object. The action of each section takes place in a different part of town, but in each case the characters are a husband and a wife. The title character never appears. In some cases his physical presence offstage is indicated, but in others (after his death, for example) he is merely a spiritual presence, an influence on the two characters. The four sections, united only by the "presence" of Toño and the play's overall tone, show the relationships—sometimes hopeful, sometimes hopeless, usually melancholy—of each couple. The play's essence is more difficult to describe because there are so many possibilities, but no real plot.

The four acts suggest Toño's beginning, his success, his decline, and his death, but they do not come in that order. Nor do they come in order of the seasons, nor according to a clockwise or counterclockwise sequence of the points of the compass. Yet the mere fact that those sequences exist makes it possible and even necessary to consider them. The play consists of the four acts and their various elements in the order presented, as well as the multiple combinations of the elements in other various and seemingly logical combinations. The very fact of so many pieces placed out of their normal, logical, or expected order encourages their formation into some sort of order, and this act of combining provides the dynamism and inner movement in the play. In this case the movement grows from the illogical combinations; in previous plays it grew out of the geometrical forms suggested and from puzzles that had to be solved one piece at a time. The systems are all similar, and they indicate the complexity of Velásquez's plays. Unlike the direct messages of the plays in the first *Teatro joven de México*, these compel uncertainty and doubt about the concrete reality of a situation. These doubts became a central element of plays by the second wave of dramatists. Other important elements for the second wave were the history and culture of Mexico, and that is where Velásquez turned his attention after *Toño Basura*, in the second phase of his dramatic production.

Sobre las lunas, Vía libre, and Aunque vengas en figura distinta, Victoriano Huerta are all set in the past. The first takes place in 1888, on the day Porfirio Díaz dedicated the Mexican national railroad. Not surprisingly, the dictator does not appear. The play deals instead with the daughter of a government official, her suitor Gabriel, and her nanny. Nothing really happens—the daughter has lost a ruby from one of her earrings, eventually she rejects the suitor, and the sole setting is a balcony overlooking the ball celebrating the grand moment and the presence of Díaz. Nothing else is very clear, which seems appropriate, since much of the imagery relates to vision. The daughter, Asunción, besides being confined to a wheelchair, has poor vision, although vanity keeps her from wearing her glasses; one of Gabriel's eyelids sags, due to a damaged nerve; La Nana spends much of the play searching for the lost ruby, which she never finds, and looking the other way when Gabriel comes to call. The play forces a similar difficulty on the audience by being so hazy about what could really be going on here—why Asunción rejects Gabriel, the importance of the lost ruby, and the role of the nanny, which seems to be central. At the end the nanny reveals that she has had two children with Asunción's father, that he found the lost ruby and gave it to her, and that she then tried to give it away to someone in the street. Her revelations provide an explanation for only some of the play's mysteries, though, so the viewer still does not see all the events and relationships clearly.

The tone of the play produces a comment on Mexican society during the last part of the nineteenth century. There is a feeling of loneliness, separation, and sadness, and there are numerous instances of good tempered by bad: light surrounded by darkness; the presence of one ruby, but the absence of its pair; the festive dance in which Asunción cannot or will not participate; Asunción's comment as she observes the people, "¡Muerte y diversión van de la mano!" (104). This combination of good and bad could well describe the years of the *Porfiriato*, and in the end the play communicates that feeling above all. The difficulty of the play reflects Velásquez's movement from recognizable to hermetic works, the trajectory mentioned before as a trait of cubism. That trend continued in the last two plays.

The epigraph to *Vía libre* is from Ermilo Abreu Gómez's *Canek*: "—Y así aprendí—concluyó Canek—a leer, no la letra, sino el espíritu de la letra de todas esas historias" (56). A reader or viewer must adopt a similar course of action when confronted with the play. The thirteen scenes deal with the rail strikes in Mexico in 1958 and 1959, yet relatively few of the scenes present events directly related to the strikes, and even in those cases the action grows out of conflicts and relations at the level of character more than of historical events. While the play does supply a feel for what happened, the battle waged by the workers against the railroad is really the battle that all people wage against life.

Despite the use of slides, placards and signs, sound effects, stylized suggestions of sets, and scenes that apparently have no direct connection with the rest of the play (a little boy calls to his parents in the night because he has wet the bed; the mother tells him to sleep with his head at the foot of the bed), there is a kind of realism present that affects one's understanding of the events. The readers or spectators frequently are thrown into the middle of the action with little or no idea of its origin or connection to the rest of the play. The characters talk among themselves without the common dramatic convention of explaining indirectly what they are talking about for the benefit of the spectators—they simply talk. The effect is that of overhearing parts of conversations in some public place and having to imagine the related circumstances. Velásquez provided multiple bits and pieces, sometimes with obvious connections and sometimes not, and it is the viewer's job to put them together to form a whole picture, which many times turns out to be only a vague feeling about the events at hand. Yet it is this feeling that helps in understanding the essence of the events instead of merely seeing their surface. These are the puzzles that lie at the foundation of all of Velásquez's theater.

Aunque vengas en figura distinta, Victoriano Huerta continues in that same vein. The main character is the Mexican general and President, along with three other Huertas at different ages, all of whom appear on stage at the same time at various points throughout the play. The action takes place between 1869 and 1915, in Mexico, Spain, and the United States, and follows Huerta from his entry into the army, through his time as a general during the Mexican revolution, his takeover of the government from Madero, and, after his exile, his trip to the United States with the faint hope of again becoming President.

The focus on historical events and the questioning of reality predominate here. In *Tropics of Discourse* Hayden White spoke of "a fiction of the historian" (98) and said, "Historians may not like to think of their works as translations of fact into fictions; but this is one of the effects of their works" (92). This is somewhat the direction that Velásquez took, as evidenced by his introductory note: "La acción dramática reordenó el hecho histórico, por tanto, el lugar, el tiempo o los personajes, a ratos—los menos—, son equivalentes. Si se quiere, las licencias pueden consignarse en el programa de mano—tres palabras bastan: obra histórica licenciosa—; también puede prohibirse la entrada a los historiadores—sin embargo, hay mucho de historia" (15).

The main point of contention is the depiction of Huerta himself, who has been portrayed in other places as "half savage and a butcher; habitual drunkard; perfidious and perhaps fanatic; over-excited, transforming audacity into insanity; devoid of all private virtue" (Sherman and Greenleaf, 89). Eugenia Meyer's *Prólogo* to the play also notes that Huerta has been characterized as a traitor, an assassin, and an alcoholic (10). Clearly Velásquez was aware of that commonly-held perception of Huerta, since he included two pages of historical references at the end of the play. Nevertheless, this Huerta does not fall into such extremes. He does drink, he deceives Madero, and he can act arbitrarily, but one would certainly not come away from the play picturing him as an insane, butchering traitor. Huerta himself raises the question of identity in the first scene, and the question hangs over the rest of the play.

Huerta is seen in broad terms, not so much self-serving as caught in the battle between the eagle and the serpent, the battle that will determine Mexico's soul, the struggle symbolized by Yurianaka, an Indian woman who appears on stage but never speaks. "Yurianaka, la diosa de la tierra, según nosotros los mexicanos . . . Patria y tierra, Yurianaka" (18). Huerta sees himself as one who can save *patria y tierra* from the serpent, so his concerns are naturally power and control and he pursues them both from the outset in the belief that he is following the right course. This added perspective helps to round out Huerta's character and tone down the vicious madman that so many people consider him to have been.

Dramatically the structure once agains plays a part in conveying the themes, if power and control are considered central to the play. Huerta appears first as a youngster in 1869, then in his prime prior to his ascendency to the presidency, and finally old but still determined as he contemplates a return to Mexico after his exile, but the order of the sixteen scenes is decidedly not chronological. Knowing Velásquez's predilection for intricate structuring, one feels the temptation to try to make sense of the sequence of the scenes, to impose order on the apparently chaotic presentation, and to establish some sort of control. Such attempts produce as much frustration for the reader or spectator as Huerta's attempts to establish control in Mexico do for him. The fact is, the fragmented chronology and the "extra" characters serve to create the play's tone and atmosphere. *Aunque vengas en figura distinta, Victoriano Huerta* is about the historical character, but it is also a picture of the time with all its chaos crying out for order. The *figura distinta*, then, refers to more than just the four Huertas that appear in the play, because Victoriano

Huerta becomes an image that conveys many different senses. These are the true *figuras distintas* in the play.

During this five-year "lull" there was a great increase in the complication of themes and their presentation, particularly in Velásquez's work. The themes moved from a relatively narrow view of the problems of Mexico and its teenagers, as seen from their point of view, to a focus on Mexico's past. Here Velásquez continued a direction that Willebaldo López established earlier: to understand Mexico's present reality and to question common perceptions of that reality by raising doubts about accepted realities of the past. As in the case of Oscar Villegas's works, the form pulls the reader or spectator into the dramatic process because the fragmentation, the lack of chronological order, and the multiple levels of imagery force active participation if the actions are to be understood. Reality may not be what people think it is, and therefore they are almost obliged to question the world around them. That task is far removed from passively hearing that the bureaucracy is "bad".

Questioning became a fundamental characteristic of the most effective drama in the second wave. After López and Villegas and later Velásquez anticipated this approach, it simply took time for others to discover it for themselves. Before proceeding to those playwrights in the second wave, however, two dramatists from the first wave remain to be discussed.

5. The Storm Surrounding the Lull
González Dávila and Olmos

By far the largest number of this generation's writers falls into one of two groups: those who began writing before 1974 and then gradually stopped, and those who began writing after 1978. Only a few belong to the five-year period of reduced activity between 1974 and 1978. Only two began their production during the first period and continued writing after the five-year lull. Jesús González Dávila and Carlos Olmos stand apart from the other dramatists of this generation not only in that they continued to write when so many others stopped, but also in the very nature of their plays, which are unlike most of what has been considered to this point.

Both dramatists wrote about escape—futile but incessant attempts to run away from the frightening and often brutal reality that surrounds people. González Dávila expressed these ideas in widely varying types of theater, running the gamut from stylized, lyrical language to myth structure, absurdism, children's theater, and something close to theater of cruelty. His primary interest was young children and the hell in which they are forced to live and from which they try to escape. In the chronological development of González Dávila's production, this hell gradually expands to include all of humanity, not just the children, in his dark, pessimistic world. Carlos Olmos's characters also try to escape—from the past, from destiny, from rotting love, and from reality. All conspire to fashion a hellish place not unlike

González Dávila's creation, which in the end turns out to be the people themselves and the reality they create as they try to run away from that "other" reality, the "real" one. The inhabitants of Olmos's world are as unhappy as those of González Dávila's, but the darkness is somewhat mitigated by the undercurrent of black humor that runs through Olmos's work. González Dávila and Olmos worked with broader themes than did most of their contemporaries, and they presented them much more powerfully.

Jesús González Dávila

Although González Dávila began writing at about the same time as the other writers of the generation's first wave of dramatists and even had one of his plays included in the first *Teatro joven de México*, his work has little in common with other plays of the time. He generally did not concern himself with the trials of teenagers, and his characters suffer from more than merely parents' arbitrary rules. Theirs is an almost existential suffering communicated with great impact due, in part, to what Philip Wheelwright calls "tensive language." While most of his contemporaries employed realistic language in their works, González Dávila wrote plays filled with imagery and symbolism set against a mythic and/or an absurdist backdrop. No one else except Oscar Villegas produced this kind of play in which the spotlight falls not on individual characters but on a language and tone that force the audience to focus on thematic expression and not the action in and of itself.

González Dávila's first works—those written before the five-year lull—exhibit these characteristics. The same economic and artistic considerations that afflicted his fellow writers, also affected him, and after 1972 he stopped writing for a time, then turned to children's theater (*teatro infantil*) until 1981, when his children's plays became so violent that they seemed fit only for adults. As he began writing again, with the second wave of dramatists, González Dávila moved toward more realism in language, settings, and situation, and his main characters more frequently were teenagers. Still, with one exception, these works do not fall into the typical category of teenage lament plays due to the tensive language. In addition, they are set against the background of a 1970 play, *La fábrica de los juguetes*, that provides insights to the ultimate destination of those characters who are so intent on escaping their present unsatisfactory reality. The imagery in these later plays is less dense than in previous works, but González Dávila added an element of mystery (somewhat similar to what Gerardo Velásquez did—see Chapter 4). More important, the violence in the plays becomes almost palpable, not merely in the actions but in the language, the tone, and generally in the atmosphere that portrays the brutality of life.

Wheelwright, speaking of tensive language in *Metaphor and Reality*, provided a description that fits González Dávila's concerns: "As man gropes to express his complex nature and his sense of the complex world, he seeks or creates representational and expressive forms (the two adjectives standing for complementary aspects of a single endeavor) which shall give some hint, always finally insufficient, of the turbulent moods within and the turbulent world of qualities and forces, promises and threats, outside him" (46).

This turbulence, so evident in Mexico during and after 1968, concerned most of the first-wave dramatists, and they generally expressed their discontent with society openly and directly. In González Dávila's case, the turbulence is woven into the language, since the actions in his early plays seldom represent a recognizable, everyday reality. Instead he used myth and absurdism.

The title of one of González Dávila's first plays, *La venturina*, refers to a "piedra de la felicidad" (19), sought after by Rock. The entire play, in fact, is about searches. The boy, Rock, searches for *la venturina*; a younger girl, Isa, searches for butterflies, which symbolize sexual experience; Don, an older man and storyteller, searches for Rock after the latter runs off with Bella, the temptress. As the play begins, Don is telling Rock and Isa a story. Bella appears and lures Rock away, and Don and Isa follow. Bella soon abandons Rock, but he pursues her and his *venturina*. Everyone's quest succeeds, but the victories seem somewhat hollow. Rock finds the *venturina*, which is only a piece of broken glass. Don finds Rock, who dies at Bella's hands. Isa destroys the living butterflies she finds and contents herself with plastic ones instead.

The play's structure describes a failed myth cycle (see Chapter 4 for an explanation of the cycle). Rock's exit with Bella at the beginning of the play signals the "Departure," in which Don and Isa also participate. The "Trials" involve Rock's pursuit of Bella when she tires of him, Don's dealings with her, and Isa's attempts to find a group of boys associated with the butterflies. The cycle partially breaks down at the "Return," since Bella kills Rock. Still, Isa can take Bella's place as the destructive temptress in the next cycle, and Don restarts the cycle by looking to the audience for other listeners to his stories.

The themes here vaguely recall those expressed by other dramatists: the search or the hope for *something*—be it happiness, freedom, or love—leads to nothing but deception. The depth of expression, the stylization, the density of the language and symbolic expression, the myth structure, and the absence of a base in realism, however, lend the play a universal aspect that does not limit it to a specific situation in Mexico. In González Dávila's continuing search for expression, he selected some of these elements and then grounded them in absurdism in *Los gatos*.

This play pits materialism against freedom and happiness as Coni, a businesswoman, searches for a bus with no fixed route; Vera and Palo live in a newsstand that sells only old, out-of-date magazines; Din and Don give Coni a treasured cat in exchange for several months' rent; and Dario searches for his dead father's treasure box. At the end most of them are happy with their object of value (much like Rock, who dies happy), but at the expense of something else of personal importance. Din and Don give up the cat they love and Dario leaves his father in the room where he has been boarded up, unburied, for months. The play comes in fragments, seemingly disconnected poems, and absurdist dialogue. In combination they force the audience to focus on the presentation instead of the sequence of actions, similar to what Martin Esslin described in *The Theatre of the Absurd*: "The total action of the play, instead of proceeding from point A to point B, as in other dramatic conventions, gradually builds up the complex pattern of the *poetic image* that the play expresses. The

spectator's suspense consists in waiting for the gradual completion of this pattern which will enable him to see the image as a
whole. And only when that image is assembled—after the final
curtain—can he *begin* to explore, not so much its meaning as its
structure, texture, and impact" (366; the italics are Esslin's). That
impact has a great deal to do with futile and empty searches for
things not found or for things that, when found, have little or
no real value.

If the world is indeed built on futile searches, then there is a
certain hopelessness to dreams and desires. *La fábrica de los juguetes* describes the end result of the hopeless searches. The play
resembles an extended poem because of the denseness of the
imagery and the lyricism that is almost at the expense of plot.
It contains a chorus, bits and pieces of English, music, references
to the Beatles, and absurdist sections. In and of itself the play
remains extremely hermetic, but its importance lies in the key
it provides for most of González Dávila's later production.

The "factory" of the title is a dark, enclosed place where those
inside—children—spend their time waiting for the sun. There
are three groups of characters: two young children (Mar and
Flor) who have just arrived and appear to be the next who will
be trapped in the factory, several young people who have hopes
of leaving soon, and the adults who are outside. As an image
the *fábrica* has various possibilities. It is a kind of purgatory to
which the children escape while they wait their turn to leave for
what they suppose is a kind of heaven. They are referred to as
muertos (76) and *espíritus* (78), and one of them mentions a "Paraíso del Sol. Allá es donde pronto vamos a llegar" (67). The
factory could also represent the womb, where they wait for their
moment of entry into the world. The inside-outside dichotomy
also suggests the young people's perception that they are trapped, due to hints at the violence in Tlatelolco: "dispararon muchos tiros . . . rebotando entre los edificios" (73); "[El país]
. . . esa cosa loca, que se provoca, que se desboca" (82). Late in
the play, Mar and Flor offer another explanation:

Esta es la fábrica de los juguetes.
Jugando a los fantasmas. Hace juguetes.
Es como el fantasma de una fábrica

con fantasmas adentro.
Sólo una fábrica fantasma que fabrica
fantasmas de juguete. [91]

The cyclical nature of the structure recalls Joseph Campbell's "Universal Round" or "Cosmogonic Cycle," the movement between the light of waking and the dark of dreaming, a movement "represented as repeating itself, world without end" (261). This "cosmogonic cycle" consists of three planes of being: Waking, Dream, and Deep Sleep (266). These three planes suggest this possible arrangement of the elements in the play:

Waking	Dream	Deep Sleep
birth	life	death
children	teenagers	adults
next inhabitants	waiting to leave	the end

The last term under "Deep Sleep" arises from the preoccupations of the adults, one of whom swears that her "Iglesia del Perpetuo Socorro" has literally vanished (83), and another who says that "la delegación, donde trabajo" (84) has suffered the same fate. The two locations mentioned represent, significantly, two of society's fundamental bases, the church and the government.

The *fábrica* really turns out to be all of these places and states. In sum it is a horrible place where the young are dumped or to which they escape as they flee from their previous miserable circumstances. The message sounds familiar, but the presentation is nothing like what is found in other plays of the period. In addition, González Dávila showed the most compassion for the youngest children, the ones for whom he began to write plays five years later. He devoted himself to his *teatro infantil* until 1981, when he discovered that his original themes had crept back in to such an extent that his children's plays had become adults' plays once again.

The three plays that comprise *Los niños prohibidos* help to understand the importance of the *fábrica*. The point of view is that of the children and, in accordance with the play's subtitle, "Pieza negra," they find themselves enclosed in small, dark spaces. *El padrino de las mentiras* begins with a boy in an elevator, on his way to his godfather's office. The godfather and the boy's mother are ex-lovers. The boy is a liar, because he has discovered that adults think it cute: "Decir mentiras es como cuando juegas. Tú sabes que el juego es inventado, pero juegas a que es cierto aunque sea mentira. Y quien te ve no se enoja. 'Es que está jugando el niño,' dicen" (p. III). In the office the boy invents "stories" again and again and again, until the godfather becomes frustrated with him. One of the stories, though, is about a note that his mother wrote, a note that says only "Adios," and that he found (and assumed to be for the godfather) after his mother was taken away. Could it have been a suicide note? The question cannot be answered since the boy has erased the line between lies and truth. A final irony comes when the godfather becomes so frustrated at the boy's stories that he grabs him, ties his hands, and beats him. Then as he speaks on the phone, he tells the caller, "Aquí, jugando con mi ahijado. Ya sabes cómo son los niños, nunca se cansan de jugar" (p. VI). The message in this play is that adults and their lies create children and their lies, but the children get trapped in the world of adult lies, where they become toys for the stronger, more accomplished elders. This is the first sense in which children become *juguetes*, products of the factory.

Una niña muy mala y un empleado muy ocupado shows how children then come to be inhabitants of the *fábrica*. It is a short step, since from the outset both the *niña* and the father acknowledge that she is a *muñeca*. A dimly recalled woman left the girl in a box on the father's doorstep one Christmas—"Y dentro venía un regalo: ¡Una muñeca! . . . Me la mandó una amiga ocasional. De esas amigas que conoces en una borrachera y ni te vuelves a acordar. Hasta que te manda un regalito" (p. VIII)—and now he is stuck with her. The stage is divided into two areas: the girl's room, where she must remain until she finishes all of her soup, and outside her door, where her father must remain, unable to attend a party because of the girl, whom he would prefer to lock away literally and forget, like a toy in a toy box. As he sits outside imagining what the party is like, the girl inside plays at rebellion and escape from her "box": "No soy una muñeca. No soy mala. Soy simplemente una niña . . . Voy a buscar un lugar donde no regañen a las niñas malas por ser como son" (p. X). What is this place? The most likely answer is the *fábrica*, the final destination for such false hopes and useless searches for happiness. The situation is saddest and most hopeless for the children, but adults also find themselves trapped—thus the parallelism of the title.

A little girl and a nurse or social worker appear in *Una niña. Se columpiaba*. Angelina, the social worker, takes her shift watching over the girl, who apparently is in a hospital although it is never clear why her parents have put her there. Nevertheless she must stay in her small dark room. Angelina is pregnant, and the boyfriend wants nothing to do with her. Both characters are trapped, with no control over their situations. Instead they can only play at freedom, happiness, and escape. Angelina pretends to have a conversation with a friend; the girl first refuses to take her pills, then tries to take too many, and later becomes so frantic that Angelina must put her in a straight-jacket. Both of them are playthings, toys shut away in a private hell, much like the "factory." This play features the typical unwanted pregnancy, but unlike the girls in the plays from the first wave, whose response is to run away from parents who will not understand, Angelina is older, truly alone, and driven to a self-destructive anguish that only becomes worse, for her and for González Dávila's other characters.

Beginning in 1983 González Dávila dropped his stylized, symbolic, dense style and began to use more realistic language, situations, characters, and actions, pushing the action in particular to extremes. *De la calle* features a whole gallery of characters who live on the streets of Mexico City. The focus is on Rufino, who dodges the police and brutal past associates as he searches for his father. The play is realistic in its characters and in its depiction of their life and street language. The fifteen fragments follow Rufino in his search, and create a vivid image of the violent and uncontrolled world of those who live in the streets.

Trilogía continues the social realism and backgrounds its three plays with the specter of Tlatelolco. The characters in *Muchacha del alma* are very reminiscent of the stereotypical hip-talking, long-suffering teenagers and the sex-crazed males of the earliest plays of the generation. The situation and characters are more interesting in *Pastel de zarzamoras*, where a homosexual son hopes to explain to his parents why he is going to leave home and go to San Francisco with his lover. *El jardín de las delicias* is the most violent play in the collection. Two young people, Leopoldo and Luisa, have run away together to get married. She is suffering the effects of a badly done abortion, and as his mental state deteriorates he goes from hallucinations to violence. These last two plays are the most interesting since the characters and situations are not stereotypical.

At the center of *Pastel de zarzamoras* is a family in pieces because of a familiar enemy: a domineering father. The daughter has run away, apparently because of his advances toward her. One son, a student rebel who was turned in to the authorities by the father, may be in an asylum. The other son still lives at home, and the play's mystery revolves around him. He is homosexual and has brought his lover home to announce that the two of them plan to go to San Francisco together. On an earlier occasion, the first time the father had a hint of his son's homosexuality, he stuck a pistol in the boy's mouth and threatened to pull the trigger. This time he becomes so violent that he suffers an attack and collapses, although it is not clear if the attack is caused by a weak heart or extreme alcoholism. While the boy wants to be the third child to flee the home, the mother has already found her escape. She remains outside most of the central action of the play because her mind floats in its own inner reality, a circumstance underscored by the recurring image of water throughout the play. For example she stays perplexed at how the canary managed to escape, even though she constantly opens and closes the near-by window, symbolic of her own desire to escape. With the hint of the father's death, though, both she and the son can only sit waiting for the doctor. She falls deeper into her own private world, while the boy's future remains uncertain.

In González Dávila's plays the tremendous potential violence that lurks just beneath the surface plays a significant role in determining the situation of these individuals, of the family as a whole, of society, and by extension of the country itself. That violence, which more and more resembles Artaud's "theater of cruelty," first appeared in *Los niños prohibidos* and explodes in

El jardín de las delicias. In this case a mixture of reality and possibly psychotic memories and visions are laid against a backdrop of yet another awful home and another hated, domineering father.[1]

Leopoldo and his girlfriend Luisa check into a cheap hotel to await their escape from Mexico City on the morning bus. Leopoldo, who previously spent time in a mental hospital, periodically sees his sister come out of a mysterious closet, where a little girl was once killed by rats after her mother locked her in and abandoned her. These scenes with the sister, which supply the background of the boy's family, must be imaginary yet they overlap with an apparently real woman—possibly his mother—waiting for him downstairs in the lobby. His relationship with Luisa, which was never strong, has been deteriorating since she, perhaps convinced by his father, had a back-alley abortion. She experiences physical pain throughout the play while Leopoldo disintegrates mentally and finally, exasperated by her moans, beats her so brutally that she soon dies. *El jardín de las delicias* provides the harshest view of the *fábrica* to which the young exile themselves. The "factory" seems faintly familiar to the Mexico City described by Leopoldo's sister: "A ver cuánto tardas en regresarte. A la mierda, al nervio, al frenesí . . . Aquí. En medio del batidero de sangre sucia, intoxicada, maloliente y lo que quieras" (80-81).

The hate and cruelty are almost palpable in this cheap, dirty, enclosed, half-real, half-nightmarish hell of memories, hallucinations, and pain. The play creates doubt for the audience about what is real and what is imagined, but that aspect is less important than the attack on the audience's sensibilities. The extreme mental and physical violence enacted onstage create the effects proposed by Artaud in his theater of cruelty. Artaud wrote, "We are not free. And the sky can still fall on our heads. And the theater has been created to teach us that first of all" (79). He continued, "I propose then a theater in which violent physical images crush and hypnotize the sensibility of the spectator seized by the theater as by a whirlwind of higher forces" (82-83). *El jardín de las delicias* in particular produces these forces.

From the lyricism and stylized death in the mythic *La venturina*, the violence in González Dávila's dramatic world—his factory—grew enormously. He defined the factory in 1970, but was forced to set its nightmares aside because of economic considerations. The essence of the factory sat waiting and growing as he wrote his *teatro infantil*, until it apparently become too powerful to contain in *Los niños prohibidos* of 1981. Then it came spilling out, all the violence and brutality of life grounded in a reality where all hopes for happiness and escape from prison cells lead only to more violence and brutality in the *Fábrica de los juguetes*, where everyone is condemned to play dark, destructive games in the storms of Jesús González Dávila's dark, destructive world.

Carlos Olmos

In describing why certain dramatists were not included in the first *Teatro joven de México*, Emilio Carballido explained, "Pilar Retes, Carlos Olmos, deberían estar aquí: no tenían obras cortas" (16). Olmos started writing at the same time as others in the first wave of dramatists, and in that sense he should be included with them. At the same time, he does not really belong, as Carballido mentioned. Even though some of his concerns may be similar, his style and the look and feel of his plays are quite different. He is also one of the few dramatists who wrote before, during, and after the five-year lull.

Like González Dávila, Olmos built his dramatic world around the desire to escape. Unlike González Dávila, his characters try to escape from destiny not by fleeing into the "factory," but by creating an alternative reality in which to live. This created reality is a nebulous concept and, depending on one's perspective, can be more or less "real" than the original reality. At times, in the characters' minds, their creations become more concrete than and take the place of the reality of the world that surrounds them. Many times it turns out to be as bad or perhaps worse, but that does not stop the futile search for a way to escape.

The theme of creating reality begins immediately with Olmos's first play, the intriguing *Lenguas muertas*. Beatriz, the wife and narrator, tells the story of Luciano who has the gift of storytelling, an art he uses to earn a living. Luciano's dreams begin to be invaded by "sombras de blanco" (16), which show him the future. Blessed with this new ability he opens a storytelling club which puts him in direct competition with the priest and the church. His ability to weave the future into his stories turns him into a kind of god for the people and increases his earnings dramatically. People begin to pay him to tell stories that do things—such as kill their rivals—while the potential victims pay even more to *not* be killed. The most dangerous request concerns a revolution planned by the Colonel, who will take over the government after one of Luciano's stories "kills" the Governor. Luciano, of course, does not have the ability to do that, so he plans to leave town, but the priest, in a battle not only for the town but for Beatriz's soul as well, reveals Luciano's deceit. A riot ensues, several people, including Luciano, are killed, and Beatriz goes crazy and becomes the only person in the town who dares to speak after the episode is over. Everyone else falls into total silence.

The play deals with the ability to change destiny and power and its effects. Can people change destiny? To Beatriz at least, Luciano claims they cannot, yet he realizes that as far as the townspeople are concerned, he is God. Beatriz tells him, "¡Tendrías que ser Dios!" and Luciano responds, "En el pueblo lo soy" (53). One's power and ability, then, depend to an extent on the perception of others. Luciano does bring change: he turns from a simple storyteller into a godlike being, he releases the hatred in the people, and his "gift" transforms Beatriz from a woman who is frustrated by his refusal to engage in sex with her to a mystical believer who insists that he maintain his purity. Olmos shows how power, whether real or perceived, changes not only those who believe in it or accept it, but also those who "possess" it. Given the right circumstances, reality can be created. This theme is part of what sets Olmos apart from most of his contemporaries. It also presages what came in his later plays.

The collection *Tríptico de juegos* features games and reality. Some games are intended to escape from reality, others to create a new one, and still others to maintain an old one. The three plays also deal with the lack of love, both family and romantic. *Juegos profanos* lays out a story of incest between brother and sister, of their Electra and Oedipus complexes, and the destiny inherent in family. The play turns in on itself due to the doubts it creates for the viewer or reader. Either the parents kill the children when the incest is discovered, or the brother and sister, who love mother and father respectively, effectively transform themselves into the father and the mother so they can "legitimately" love each other, then kill the real parents. In any case, Saúl and Alma live with skeletons (literally), supposedly of the parents, and engage in confusing conversations in which they speak for themselves or for either parent, without much indication as to who is speaking. At one point Saúl responds to something his sister has said: "¡Alma!" She then replies, "¡Está hablando papá, bruto!" (25). If the characters cannot tell the difference, the audience surely cannot.

The tension increases rapidly as they suggest that they did kill their parents years before (28), repeat the scene when they confessed their incestuous relationship, lament "un amor original lleno de gusanos y de moscas" (39), and agree to a suicide pact. When Saúl empties a pistol point-blank at his sister's head, though, the bullets produce no effect. Failing in that attempt to end their existence, they merely take on another one. They decide to exchange clothes with the skeletons, which they had previously thrown aside ("killed"), thus "becoming" the parents. Are Alma and Saúl the children or the parents, and who killed whom?

The question is unanswerable and probably unimportant since, in Olmos's world, reality is mainly invented. The real is indistinguishable from the false, except that "real" reality is destiny and inescapable. This is shown in *Lenguas muertas* at the level of society and here at the level of family and heritage. The characters begin by pretending that they can create alternatives to reality and destiny, and soon lose sight of the difference between what is real and what is invented. They get so caught up in the game that, apparently, the difference ceases to matter. Olmos's plays show this over and over, and they show it in a myriad of ways. In *Juegos impuros* Mab says, "Imaginar . . . siempre imaginar . . . hay veces en que pienso que lo único real . . . " (51). As a result of this there are consequences: "¡Hay más infiernos en ti que los que quieres encontrar bajo la tierra!" (50-51). The hell that people bring on themselves turns out to be worse than the "real" hell (that they imagine exists).

Juegos fatuos shows this very clearly. Two women—Carmen

and her nanny Tila—have spent most of their lives alone. Twenty years earlier Carmen's father ran off the men they hoped to marry, and the women have waited all that time, imagining that the men will eventually return. The women know they are playing and that the neighbors consider them crazy, but the games have gone on for so long that they have become overpowering: "Si tú lograras comprender cómo nos cambia el juego" (66); "¡O seguimos jugando, o ellos dejarán de pertenecernos para siempre!" (68); "El juego nos da fuerza, voluntad" (68). Carmen, who wants to stop playing, suggests that the game is "una creencia" (68), and Tila asks her, "¿Y quién puede decirnos que estar vivas, que estar aquí, no es otra creencia más?" (68). The game tortures Carmen, and she understands that they cannot really change the past, yet the power they do have is surprising: although the stage directions indicate that the first act takes place in the morning (58), Tila says, "¡Es de noche porque así lo queremos!" (76). So, one more time, they create the marriage party, and this time the false becomes true. Carmen "has" her husband with her and is finally married. This will leave Tila alone, and she protests, "¡Niña, por favor, es una locura!" to which Carmen responds, "¡Tú quieres engañarme! ¡Eres tú la que está loca! ¡La que me obligaste a esto! ¡Me hiciste creer en lo que no existía, Tila!" (107). Carmen knows that they are playing, and that her new reality is false, but it is so real that it no longer matters.

The game has driven Carmen to a state that could be described as insanity, but she is sane enough to know that she is acting insane. This leaves her in a shadowy middle ground where fiction is more powerful than reality and destiny. While people cannot escape reality literally, they can pretend they have, but often it is only an escape to something worse.

As Olmos continued his writing into the period of the second wave, he maintained these themes, but more and more began to focus on the power of the word. He began with the absurdist *Las ruinas de Babilonia* in which Momo creates crossword puzzles. One day when Lala asks him for the final answer, Momo does not know what it is, and their world of words falls apart. The world and the past come undone because, if words equal reality and the search for words becomes futile, then reality disappears.

Reality can also be thrown away. In *La rosa de oro* a socially conscious poet goes to collect a prize—a large sum of money and a gold-plated rose—that a book of his poetry has won for him. He declares that, "¡La misión que tengo en esta vida es descubrir la Belleza y la Verdad!" (154). Unfortunately neither appears to exist, and he finds himself instead with "mi soledad, mi angustia" (182). He compounds his plight with his materialism as he borrows beer money and continues to lament. The play offers up almost total cynicism. The characters find nothing of value, they are almost all caricatures, and no one believes in anything—not beauty or truth, not laws or cosmic revelations, not poetry or power. Nothing works, everyone is unhappy, there are no sympathetic characters, and almost no plot to speak of. The poet comes for his prize, everyone anguishes, and he gives both the money and the rose away. Everything is empty, much as in Olmos's latest play, El brillo de la ausencia (1982).

With El brillo Olmos adds a social element and a touch of black humor to a situation that recalls Juegos fatuos. Here a mutually created fantasy becomes reality. The four characters are in Paris, having escaped from Mexico after engaging in terrorist activities. Miguel is a writer; Sonia is there to be near her long-lost daughter; Raymundo is a teacher; Annie, who is with Raymundo, wants to have children but so far has only had imagined pregnancies. The other three are as empty as the childless Annie. Raymundo has no classes to teach; there is some doubt that Sonia's daughter even exists, much less in Paris where the group lives; and Miguel is only *trying* to write a book, having produced nothing up to this point.

Little by little it is revealed that they are not in Paris at all. In part they are helping Miguel with his book—"¡Nos pidió que le hiciéramos atmósfera para escribir! ¡Así empezó todo!" (261)—but they do not even play very well, since the invention occasionally breaks down: Annie says, "Dios mío . . . a veces me pierdo . . . me confundo en todo esto" (243). Still, they keep trying and insisting that, "¡La realidad es lo que tú quieras!" (278); "Son cosas que podrían pasarnos" (260). That is not really true because these four are too afraid of the real world to confront it, much less to be terrorists. Instead they hide from the Mexico that they can see just outside their window.

Even though Sonia says that she wants to stop playing, they

have to continue because they cannot or do not want to face reality. They are also too weak to protest against it, so all they have left to do is to play at being terrorists, at being exiles in Paris, and at having abortions to explain their lack of children. They play at escaping from what they imagine is a horrible reality and then increase the horror. Their fantasy is far worse than reality, but they at least think they can control it while they cannot even face reality. They find themselves left with nothing at all.

Both Jesús González Dávila and Carlos Olmos show a reality so awful that the first instinct is to escape from it by creating alternatives. But the alternatives do not lead to anything better, and sometimes do not lead to anything at all. González Dávila's characters end up in the *fábrica*, condemned to a living death in a hell that is as violent, brutal, and cruel as the world from which they escaped. As for Olmos's characters, they create alternate realities that turn out to be as bad or worse than "real" reality.

González Dávila and Olmos differ from most of their contemporaries, at least in part, because their settings are not specifically Mexican. Although they offer a comment on society, it is a more global society. The communication of their negative, pessimistic view of the world is as important as the commentary itself. Their message is delivered with a power that assaults the spectators as much or more than the stormy reality from which the characters are trying to escape. It may be this power that kept them writing long after many of their contemporaries gave up the struggle. Unlike their characters, Jesús González Dávila and Carlos Olmos chose to battle the storms of life, not to escape from them.

6. Many Realities
Berman and Espinosa

The seven-year period from 1967 to 1973 that constitutes the first wave of new Mexican drama produced some fifty plays by a dozen or so playwrights, most of whom stopped writing after a few years. The second wave, corresponding to the seven years from 1979 to 1985, produced double that number of plays and well over two dozen new, active dramatists. The growth came not only in numbers but also in the overall quality of the plays. Although many of the themes remained similar, their presentation gained more depth and variety and began to be couched in full-length form (as opposed to the previously more common short one-acts), and several writers appeared whose work consistently maintained a high level of interest and excellence throughout the period. It is debatable whether greater public acceptance—stagings and publication in the Universidad Autónoma Metropolitana's *Nueva Dramaturgia Mexicana* series, and collections and anthologies by Editores Mexicanos Unidos—encouraged writers to continue working, or whether the plays' higher quality opened more doors. There was undoubtedly some movement in both directions.

The dramas themselves lent scant attention to the sufferings of teenagers. Instead, their scope widened to address the condition of Mexico in the 1980s and the approaches multiplied along with the number of writers and plays. Dramatists foraged through Mexico's history, culture, folklore, and myths searching out explanations for the current state of affairs in the country. In this regard it is interesting to consider John Brushwood's com-

ments in *La novela mexicana (1967-1982)*. He indicated four primary characteristics in those novels: "metaficción, Tlatelolco,
novela de la ciudad e identidad inestable" (20). These same elements also characterize many of the plays already discussed.
They take place in Mexico City, suggestions of Tlatelolco lie in
the background, metatheater substitutes for metafiction, and
"unstable identity" is slowly transformed into "unstable reality." The period covered by Brushwood ended as the second
wave of dramatists began to write, and one of his observations
is particularly significant: "Ultimamente, alcanzamos a ver una
probable quinta característica, representada por una tendencia
al empleo de la novela de nostalgia, incluyendo la histórica" (20).
The mention of history is pertinent to theater. Brushwood referred approximately to the period when Gerardo Velásquez (in
1979) revived Willebaldo López's earlier experiments with historical themes, and when history, along with its attendant social
and cultural aspects, became central elements in the drama of
such writers as Sabina Berman, Tomás Espinosa, Oscar Liera,
and Victor Hugo Rascón Banda. The work of these four writers
was fundamental to the second generation and they are the focus
of the next two chapters.

The plays of both Sabina Berman and Tomás Espinosa help
to prove that reality may only be a figment of someone's imagination, and that it can be created quite easily by almost anyone. Berman mounted her attack on reality primarily by
undermining the foundation of history and suggesting that, if
people cannot trust historical reality, then their current reality
may also be in doubt. Tomás Espinosa took present-day reality,
twisted it, and had his characters create or try to substitute personal realities that seem at least as tenable. Appropriately both
dramatists undermined the idea of a concrete reality even before
opening their dramatic world. Five of the six plays in *Teatro de
Sabina Berman* have had two titles and in some cases significantly
different texts, so that spectators at *Yankee* or *Herejía*, for example,
soon discover that they are actually seeing *Bill* or *Anatema* again.
Espinosa's approach, whether intentional or not, was more personal. Aided only by his publications, it is impossible to determine if he is Tomás *Espinoza* or Tomás *Espinosa*, since both
spellings appear randomly through various publications, in-

cluding *both* forms in *Tramoya 18* and *Danza y Teatro* 7.36. The doubts about what names one should give to the two writers' reality and what constitutes their reality are indicative of what awaits the spectators or readers when they settle back with one of these plays.

Sabina Berman

In *Tropics of Discourse* Hayden White wrote, "The historical narrative does not *image* the things it indicates; it *calls to mind* images of the things it indicates, in the same way that a metaphor does" (91; the italics are White's). His view of historical works, quoted earlier in reference to the works of Gerardo Velásquez, bears repeating here: "Historians may not like to think of their works as translations of fact into fictions; but this is one of the effects of their works" (92). Sabina Berman seems not only to have subscribed to this logic, but to have taken it a few steps beyond. By pushing White's idea, one can begin to define the effect of Berman's plays. If one accepts that today's actions (facts) are tomorrow's history (that is to say, tomorrow's fiction), then one of the questions that may be asked is, at what point does the fact become the fiction? Is it nearer tomorrow, in the transcription of the fact? Is it a little closer to the present, in the recalled perceptions of the facts as they are about to be transcribed? Or is it in the present itself, in the original perception and understanding ("translation"?) of the facts? This sequence of questions brings doubt about what is real into the present moment and begins to reflect Erik Erikson's thinking.

In *Toys and Reasons* Erikson said, "There is a grim determination of adults to 'play roles'—that is, to impersonate to the point of no return their places in a cast forced upon them by what they consider inescapable reality" (18). Even if people consider their original perceptions to be reality, they will convert them into fiction ("plays"), and therefore be unable to determine what is real and what is fiction. Berman took these abstract possibilities and made them concrete in her plays.

That Sabina Berman was one of the most successful playwrights of this generation is evidenced by the fact that she won the Instituto Nacional de Bellas Artes *Premio Nacional de Teatro* for all of her major plays (*Bill/Yankee* in 1979, *Un buen trabajador del piolet/Rompecabezas* in 1981, and *Anatema/Herejía* in 1983) as well as the *Premio Nacional de Teatro para Niños* for *La maravillosa historia del chiquito Pingüica* in 1982.

There are reasons for all the multiple titles. *El jardín de las delicias* became *El suplicio del placer* when Berman gave the original title to Jesús González Dávila for one of his plays. *Esta no es una obra de teatro* was initially a final exam for director Abraham Oceransky's drama classes, but when it began to be performed commercially Berman changed the name to *Un actor se repara.* Because *Bill* did not seem to be completely meaningful to a Mexican audience, she changed the name to *Yankee* (sometimes *Yanqui*). In the case of both *Un buen trabajador del piolet* and *Anatema* vocabulary played a significant role, since neither "piolet" nor "anatema" struck recognizable chords. As a result the plays became *Rompecabezas* and *Herejía* respectively.

Apart from those anecdotal reasons, there are thematic explanations that not only justify the changes but tie them to the material contained within the plays and also to the comments offered by White and Erikson. The titles are clearly unstable (the best example being *Bill/Yankee/Yanqui*), thus providing one example of an unstable reality, or unstable identity in Brushwood's terms. The texts behind the titles have also changed (and significantly in the case of *Yankee*), thereby creating an even larger unstable reality. The unstable texts behind the unstable titles offer examples of unstable historical realities, and therefore combine present and past instability. As one works through the plays, that circle of past and present conspires to create doubts in the mind of the reader or spectator about what comprises the reality that surrounds all people.

Berman's earliest plays established that "creative acts" lead to the doubtful realities. In its use here "creative act" can be understood as a kind of play "written" by one character for himself or herself and other characters. In these plays, others are expected to participate by accepting the role and reciting the dialogue written by the first character. These alternate realities become sources of conflict that destabilize personal relationships as well as what normally passes for reality.

The first short play of the three that make up *El suplicio del*

placer features a couple who look and dress alike and have a pact
that allows both a certain amount of freedom in their outside
contacts. They are proud of their liberal views and their freedom,
but they are also unhappy. He feels guilty because, while he
picks up women, she does not pick up men. Pieces of their
dialogue as well as their similar physical appearance suggest that,
in fact, she may be more attracted to women and he to men.
The fact that he cannot remember the previous night's events
only compounds the doubts about what and who these two
characters really are. The elaborate "play" that they have written
for themselves has erased their identities instead of liberating
them.

In the second play a man sits waiting impatiently for his mistress to finish dressing. As he waits, he complains about her,
insults her, and finally begins to praise his wife for her understanding and to criticize his lover for being only a sex object,
even as he pushes her into bed. He drives himself to distraction
when he is with either one because, while they do what he tells
them to do, it is only because he has paid them (by providing
houses, fine clothes, and assorted luxuries) to act in his "play,"
not because of any real feelings. It appears that he has complete
control over his situation, yet he has none.

Similarly, the last play of the group features an aging and
bored couple's attempts to remember a dream that the wife may
or may not have had, in which she thinks the man may or may
not have brought home a pistol with which to kill her. Not only
do the characters lose track of what is real, but so do the spectators and readers. The question of why these characters feel so
compelled to create alternative realities finds an answer in *Un
actor se repara*.

The scene in this monologue is an empty stage during the
final exam in a drama class. A student actor enters, assumes the
teacher-director is sitting somewhere in the darkened audito-
rium, and tries to figure out what to do to show what he has
learned. Unfortunately he gets no help nor even any response
from the director, and the action consists of his attempts to do
something, to prove his ability, to fill the silence, and to get the
nonexistent director to give him some direction. The actor becomes increasingly frustrated and finally concludes, "Todo lo

que me enseñaste es falso, maestro . . . Todo esto es una invención de una invención: no hay nada real en este asunto, por lo
tanto todo es posible, todo aceptable y cualquier cosa que se me
ocurra llenará el vacío actual" (316). If anything is possible, then
people certainly can and possibly must determine their own
stage and stage setting, their roles, and their supporting characters, and then hope that they can convince those around them
to cooperate. These hopes and doubts form the background for
the three full-length plays in Berman's anthology.

As its title indicates, *Rompecabezas* is a riddle, a puzzle, a search
for answers. At the same time that the play reveals the questions
at the level of plot, it turns on itself and questions not only the
questions but the supposed answers. The first act depicts the
assassination of Leon Trotsky, but the drama focuses primarily
on the authorities' attempts to discover the true identity of the
murderer. Through much of the play a police investigator inter-
rogates the killer, brings in past acquaintances to identify him,
and finally allows the defense lawyer to restage the murder,
partially, it turns out, for the benefit of the press. The reenactment blatantly distorts the action already witnessed in Act I, and
it is in this respect that the play questions itself: at the same time
that it is suggesting a probable identity and explanation for the
assassin and his act, it is undermining its own suggestions with
a long series of identities and explanations that place previous
ones in doubt.

To understand how these doubts arise, it helps to begin by
accepting the absolute worth and at the same time the absolute
worthlessness of the word. For example, one of the police investigator's primary objectives in the play is to determine the
assassin's name, but by the end the investigator has discovered
five possible names, which both achieves and obscures the original goal. The killer has also been kind enough to supply a written
confession—words that establish his guilt—yet most of the facts
contained in it are false. In addition the play itself is words about
words: the opening scenes merely act out the testimony as it is
given by Trotsky's wife, the numerous interrogations are all recorded on tape, and throughout the play a secretary onstage
transcribes everything that the characters say. As a result the
play is literally "re-written" at every performance. Where, then,

among all the recordings, rewritings, and reenactments is the real play, the real action, the real event, the real history? Here one begins to tread on the ground laid by White and Erikson.

Amid this confusion lies one of the play's structural bases: the juxtaposition of singular and plural, the one truth and the many versions of it. There is one assassin (truth, reality), but five identities (fallacy). There is one murder, but in its "reproduction" the death blow is repeated several times for the photographers. The simple and eloquent "gone" (85-87; 92) spoken in English by a single unidentified woman at the hospital contrasts with several journalists' sensationalized reports of the death. These instances and more produce a set of oppositions: one and many, truth and lies, destruction and creation (that is to say, the murder on the one hand and its reconstructions in the confession, the interrogation, the reenactment, and the play itself on the other), the past event and its multiple recreations in histories, the reality and the words used to convey it, and ultimately the referent and the signifier.

This is evident at the level of literature—that is, for a spectator who is unaware of the historical facts—because *Rompecabezas* leaves the audience in doubt about the killer's identity, which is seemingly established, only to be questioned later. There are also doubts about the murder itself, since the defense lawyer's reconstruction of the crime in the third act so thoroughly distorts the original action. Surprisingly, neither the inspector nor any of the other characters object to the falsification. The reporters pour into the vacuum and finish the creation of what will be the public's accepted reality, simply because they will have read the account and seen the pictures in the newspaper.

These actions fall within the dramatic fiction, but as "history" the play creates other thorny questions because, while the work follows the historical facts very closely, at the same time it violates them by using inaccurate names for the killer and by restaging the crime so falsely.

The third act's blatantly falsified reconstruction of the crime places the original and supposedly historical depiction in Act I in doubt; from there it is a short step to further doubts about the historical accuracy of any part of the play. The clarification of those doubts should lie outside of the text, in "history books."

Interestingly enough though, a search produces not a history, but *histories*. One brief example serves to illustrate.

Among other names, the assassin in the play is called Jacques Mornard and Ramón Mercader. In a book published in 1972, the author stated, "It is almost certain, now, that Mornard was Mercader" (Mosley, 152); in a book published the following year, the authors wrote, "The true identity of 'Mornard' was never established" (Serge and Trotsky, 272). Was it or wasn't it? One man, many identities; one event, many accounts. In the numerous books on the subject, one can find a number of other, similar contradictions. In fact, in another play about Trotsky, Peter Weiss's *Trotsky in Exile*, the assassin is named "Jacson."

All of these discrepancies accumulate and eventually begin to place history in doubt. In the list of oppositions mentioned previously—one/many, truth/lies, destruction/creations, historical event/historical accounts, reality/words, referent/signifiers—the second term always makes it difficult or impossible to reach the first. The signifiers do not reveal the referents, the words hide the reality, and the accounts do not clarify the events. Insofar as historical accounts and therefore history itself are depicted, it becomes difficult to avoid wondering what is real and true. Berman depicted these doubts more graphically in *Herejía*.

This play takes place during the period of the colonization of the New World and focuses on the Carvajal family in Mexico. Here one sees a true but secret reality and a manufactured, public one, since the members of the family are Jews who are forced to practice their religion in secret and mascarade as fervent Catholics for the benefit of the Inquisition. The action traces their increasingly fanatical devotion to Judaism, which ends in their arrest and sentencing at the hands of the Inquisition. In the process Berman introduces a sequence of scenes that present one character's visions or hallucinations in parallel with "real" scenes in which the Inquisitors torture Francisca Carvajal. An angel appears to her son Luis and, in one of the frequent uses of Hebrew in the play, Luis says to the angel, "Baruj ata adonai . . . ," to which the angel replies, "Blah, blah, blah. Rezar ante un ángel es como llevar un puño de sal al mar. Ven a comer papa" (205). The angel then produces a potato, which he says represents Luis's mother, cuts it in half, and tells Luis that he (Luis) is butter, after which Luis eats his half of the potato. This vision, this distorted view brought about by Luis's suffering, is followed by a scene depicting a real event—doña Francisca's torture. The stage directions indicate: "Cámara de torturas, instantes después. Ahora el potro está vertical, con doña Francisca atada. Los verdugos en el suelo acostados, pero en posturas de estar de pie. La mesa también vertical, los inquisidores sentados en sus sillas, pero de costado al suelo. Es una vista desquiciada" (203). This sideways scene suggests that the world is twisted and distorted, and the spectator is confronted by a very "real" representation of it.

In fact, the entire process of getting to the play itself mirrors the twisted reality that Berman constantly presented. Parts of the play are based on a book by Alfonso Toro, which in turn was based on two sources: Luis de Carvajal's autobiography, which grew out of fanaticism and persecution, and the Inquisition's recorded testimony of the trial, which coincidentally is based on those same two factors. Both purport to show realities that can probably never be verified; then Berman created even more distortions around them. The deeper one looks, the more one loses sight of what is true and what is invented. Thus it becomes more and more difficult to determine if historical texts tell the "truth" since there exist so many obviously distorted historical texts. As one moves to more contemporary texts and to texts with a more contemporary basis, where does the line between distorted and non-distorted fall? If it is possible to re-create the distant past, then why not the near past and even the present? *Yankee* investigates that question.

The change in title from *Bill* to *Yankee* brought various changes to the text as well, but the plot and themes remain the same. The title character jumps ship in Puerto Vallarta and goes to work in the home of a Mexican couple, hoping that the wife can help him to collect and organize the pieces of his life.

The action of the play takes place after Bill has served in Vietnam. It is not absolutely certain that he actually went, but the strongest suggestion is that he did. One experience in particular—the killing of a woman and her child—had the harshest effect on him, leaving his personality fragmented and disconnected. When he sees Rosa and her baby in the market, he convinces himself that she is his salvation and follows her home, offering to do repairs in the house in exchange for room and board. He hopes to recreate himself through Rosa, his "Madonna," and through his portrait, to be done by her artist husband. Alberto is not a painter, however; he is a writer. In fact, he is currently working on a novel in the hope that it will win a prize. Alberto's devotion to his work has already strained his relationship with Rosa, and Bill's presence only aggravates the situation. She begins to devote more and more time to the intruder, treating him almost as her second child, and less and less to her husband, who soon begins to resent the lack of attention. The resulting tensions end with violence when, in the final scene, Bill knocks Alberto unconscious after the latter threatens to call the police.

Even as brief a synopsis as this suggests the wide variety of themes included in the play. The plot weaves together the question of personality development, love, artistic creation, and the effects of war, along with other themes, one of which—the unreliability of logic—constantly threatens to undo the others. Bill dwells on an image from an Aztec poem: "una red de agujeros" (18). It is an image that becomes his anthem and his explanation for all the faulty logic he sees around him. The lack of logic in the world shows up in the play at various times and begins to fray the edges of the textual net. Most frequently it finds its way into the play in the form of binary oppositions that refuse to remain opposed. A segment from the first scene of *Bill* (a segment that disappears in *Yankee*) demonstrates the binary breakdown.

At one point Bill asks Rosa if Elizabeth Taylor and Richard Burton were not married in Puerto Vallarta, and Rosa replies, "No sé. Dicen que por lo menos aquí se enamoraron" (*Bill*, 127). Her answer introduces the concept of love, and Bill immediately proposes its opposite with a short anecdote about the famous couple's anniversary trips to the port city: "Se perseguían por las calles oscuras gritando leperadas. 'Liz, forgive me. I won't slap you again. If I did it is because that's the way I express love.' 'Oh Richard, I run from you not because you slap me but because you don't slap good enough' " (128). For Burton then, a slap signifies love, but he assumes that for Taylor it means non-love.

He is only partially correct because while "good enough" slaps can indicate love to her, poor or imperfect slaps cannot. In this case, both opposing terms are present in a sign (the slap) that is generally considered to convey the idea of "non-love," although not the same "non-love" understood by Taylor. The anecdote sets up a false opposition because it demonstrates a single sign that signifies love, non-love, and at the same time both and neither. Love can be non-love and non-love can be love in a topsy-turvy system with fundamental contradictions that ensure failure.

The plot follows a similar pattern. It can be divided into two primary lines: Bill's attempt to recover his identity, and Alberto's attempt to write his novel. Utilizing the narrative grammar proposed by Tzvetan Todorov in *The Poetics of Prose* (108-119), these actions may be expressed as two sets of propositions:

1) Bill enters the house in order to find (recreate, perfect) himself.	1) Alberto enters the house in order to create a perfect novel.
2) Bill questions Alberto's attempt at perfect creation.	2) Alberto questions Bill's attempt to recreate (perfect) himself.
3) Bill fails (to leave his violent past behind; to convince Alberto his novel is too intellectual).	3) Alberto fails (to finish his novel; to discover Bill's identity).

The second proposition in each set holds special interest because it represents an action that strays from the active agent's specific objective and ultimately produces the conditons that doom the individual projects. Specifically, Bill offends Alberto by claiming that his novel is only paper and ink and that he is out of touch with day-to-day realities, and Alberto retaliates by questioning the authenticity of Bill's background. Both men begin to devote as much time to secondary, destructive goals as to their original, creative ones.

On a structural level the similarity between the two plots allows an important extension: their combination into one mas-

ter set of propositions, with "X" and "Y" representing the active
and passive agents respectively:

1) X (withdraws and) attempts to create (perfectly).
2) X questions (attempts to destroy) Y's perfect creation.
3) X fails (to create; to destroy).

There are two separate, active agents, but they seek a common
objective. They also seek to prevent the opposition from reaching
a goal. The two sets of propositions are separate but similar, and
in the second step of the sequence each intrudes on the other.
This scheme supports the notion that *Bill/Yankee* is a play about
failure and further suggests that the failure includes both creation and destruction. Finally, the propositions underscore the
breakdown in the system of binary oppositions, in this case creator and destroyer—mutually exclusive terms that become
fused.

At the same time that the text communicates the theme of
faulty or failed logic, it participates in it. At one moment of
conflict, for example, Rosa wonders if there are not really three
babies in the house: her son, Bill, and Alberto.

ALBERTO. Maldito gringo. Usted tiene la culpa. [Rosa] está
          harta de cuidarlo encima de tener que cuidar al
          bebé.
BILL.   Dijo: ¿a cuál de los tres niños? Usted también es
          un niño.
ALBERTO. No me hables de tú.
BILL.   Te hablé de usted. [53]

Here the text comes apart; it falls through a hole in its net, just
as Bill and Alberto fall through the holes in theirs. When it
happens to them, they turn for salvation to Rosa—the Mother,
the creator, the protector.

Rosa acts as secondary or assistant creator to the men's projects in addition to her own role of mother to the baby. Predict-
ably, she "fails" in her creative acts, just as do the men. When
Bill insists that he fled to Canada, thus ultimately becoming a
traitor and good (as opposed to having gone to Vietnam and

now being a hero and bad—another example of logic gone
awry), Rosa supports him in his hero-traitor dilemma by telling
him what he wants to hear. In this way she protects him, but
only by encouraging his illusions and inventions.

Alberto needs her to verify his creation, too, but in this case
she intentionally fails to be as perfect as her husband requires
and in so doing contributes to the decline of the power and value
of Alberto's words, which begin to deteriorate from his first encounter with Bill. In the most telling example, Rosa refuses to
listen obediently as Alberto reads her his latest chapter:

ALBERTO. ¿No quieres escucharlo? Es bueno, creo.
ROSA.   ¿Tú quieres que lo escuche?
ALBERTO. ¿Qué pasa?
ROSA.   Dios, cuánto trabajo te cuesta admitir que neces-
          itas leérmelo.
ALBERTO. Yo no necesito nada. El capítulo ya está escrito.
          Da igual que lo conozcas. [52]

So he says, but if Rosa refuses to reify his fictional world to bring
it into the real world (a birth?), the creation remains incomplete.

Even the baby represents a lapse or hole in the net. One
morning Rosa wakes and discovers, to her horror, that Bill has
taken the baby to play on the beach. She has assured Bill that
she trusts him with the baby, but her reaction belies her words.
She fears for the baby's safety and therefore has not managed
to protect it, at least as perfectly as a Madonna would. Bill and
Alberto's construction of the perfect Mother is unsuccessful,
then, for at times she chooses not to create, and other times she
protects only imperfectly.

In the play, creators always fail their creations. The pure (ino-
cente) Madonna does not protect her babies, Alberto does not
protect his novel, and Bill never fully conceptualizes even one
identity. All of their idealistic hopes for perfection lead to imperfect works, and the creators become destroyers. Even the text
"fails" to achieve perfection because from time to time it contains
a hole into which an unwary reader or spectator may fall. Seemingly the creative act includes an element of destruction. How
does one understand reality when it is composed of mutually

exclusive elements, and when the many creations hide the (supposedly) one, original creation? The created realities themselves cannot function without the full cooperation of all the participants ("characters"), which is rarely forthcoming. The recounting of history is a kind of creation; daily life also leads to the creation of realities. It is relatively easy to overlook all the duplicity since it is so common, but Berman, by confronting her audiences with the multiple realities, forces them to face concrete examples of her view of the world—of the multiple, flexible, and unstable realities that people create around them.

Tomás Espinosa

Tomás Espinosa simplified Berman's multiple realities somewhat by cataloguing them as the bad that surrounds humankind and the good that people try, usually in vain, to make of it. Espinosa's characters are trapped by the modern world, and although they might want to escape or to change it they cannot. The more they try, the more they become what they are trying to escape.

Espinosa's production can be divided into three stages. In the first the characters seek to escape from a bad situation by inventing an alternative that turns out to be worse. The characters in the plays of the second stage seem to realize that they cannot escape their circumstances, so instead of trying to run away from reality they attempt to manipulate and redistribute it. In this they seem to succeed, but their success does not really improve their condition. In the third stage it becomes clear that the manipulations are futile since the bad the characters try to change always wins, and it always wins because the characters are either already a part of it, despite their pretensions, or because they become a part of it. In Espinosa's dramatic world, then, there are only two choices: accept reality as it is or make matters worse. He communicated these ideas in plays that combine bits of realistic language and settings with characters who pull the plays toward absurdism because they are so exaggerated in their behavior.

Espinosa's first collection of short plays appeared in *Tramoya 16* under the title *Enxemplos*. These five plays along with *La televisión enterrada*, published in *Tramoya 18*, comprise the first stage in Espinosa's theater. In *El teléfono* the characters are El, Ella, and Un Teléfono. On the basis of a call that El claims was a wrong number, Ella begins to imagine what it *really* was: a call from her husband's mistress. It does not matter that it might only be a crank caller, or even that the caller was a man. The wife claims to know better: "Estoy pensando que el que habló era el hermano de tu querida"; "Estaba pensando que . . . si no era tu amante, ni un alcahuete . . . tal vez era tu hijo bastardo . . . " (7). The imagined reality and the fear that accompanies it grow until they become real enough to drive her crazy. Something similar happens in *La rata*, where a husband and wife literally tear their home apart searching for a rat that they are sure lives there. In *Angélica y Araceli*, Angélica makes it a point to be a troublemaker, even to the extent of losing her only friend. She may be exaggerating what others think of her as a defense against her fear of failure, but her actions become what in a male would be labeled obnoxious *macho* behavior. These characters respond to a bad situation by creating a worse alternative.

At times Espinosa employed signs that point in two directions at once: the male *machismo* shown in a woman and the irony of Angélica's name. In *Hacer la calle* the focus seems to be on the two main characters' homosexuality, but that becomes almost incidental. After Eloy essentially encourages and then allows Rolando to pick him up, they go to have coffee and talk. During this time the play appears to be developing into a study of a relationship between these two men, but when they get ready to leave, Eloy demands, "Págame" (16). Much to Rolando's surprise, Eloy wants to charge him for the time spent talking. When Rolando refuses, Eloy simply follows him everywhere, even to the point of (apparently) moving in with him, thus establishing the relationship, but still demanding to be paid for his time. Apparently the two men live together only because Rolando will not pay. Eloy's constant demands form the real basis for the men's relationship.

In *La televisión enterrada* a boy sets out to bury the family television set. When police and parents come looking for him, a photographer points them in another direction, and from that moment none of them can see the boy, who is standing right in front of them and who even speaks to them. Pictures, and specifically television pictures, become their reality. The parents concern themselves primarily with the *shows* that they are missing, not with the absence of their son. Logically, getting rid of the television should return sanity and humanity, but instead it eliminates the boy. In trying to destroy what constitutes his parents' reality, the boy has destroyed himself. This is the lesson in the first stage of Espinosa's drama. In the second stage, characters manipulate reality to their own liking, as shown in *Santísima la nauyaca*, Espinosa's most interesting play.

This the play consists of a series of mythical, religious, and cultural elements brought to the present day. Josefa and Isabelita are two old women who live their lives mainly through the mass media and its stars (myths), in this case "la María." The star worship mixes with religion until it essentially displaces religion. The action revolves around the reactions to the death of la María, who does not really die, despite the varying media reports of her death. There are many causes given for her death, but the most important is the bite of the poisoness *nauyaca*. The snake is *santísima* in part because it kills the star, thus allowing her fans to take over her existence and make it and her into what they choose.

There is little in the way of plot, so perhaps the most convenient way to discuss the play is by considering two characters who undergo transformations. María Cruz slowly takes on the identity of la María, and Maridalia turns into a crocodile (*yacaré*). In very general terms these two female characters represent "trapped woman" and "free woman" respectively. That description is somewhat tenuous, as is any explanation of what goes on in the play, but it seems to clarify at least the situation of each of them.

The transformations of María Cruz take on religious overtones, as suggested by her name. She is a boarder in Josefa and Isabelita's house. In the first scene, after she has awakened, she is spattered with blood. Later she enters wearing a feather boa, she is described as an "ave del paraíso," and at one point, according to the stage directions, "[María Cruz] camina en al agua" (30) (whether "on," "in," or "into," the point is made). La María belongs to and is trapped by others. As such she can exist both before and after she dies, and others are free to assume her identity. This is part of her mythic and religious status.

As myth la María both exists and does not exist. Matías Montes Huidobro detailed many of the mythic and religious elements in "Bestiario y metamorfosis en *Santísima la nauyaca* de Tomás Espinosa." His comments provide one perspective into how la María can be dead in the first two scenes, and then in the third scene attract a night club crowd to see her show. Although no one appears physically onstage each member of the audience "sees" her and is even able to provide a description of her, although the hair color ranges from black to blonde (24). What matters is that the people need la María, and they need to be able to invent the María that they prefer. It is a love-hate relationship in which she is alternately praised and condemned, at times by different people, yet also by the same person at different times. In the first scene Josefa says, "No sabía cantar, aullaba como sargento" (6), but in the club she extolls her "voz de oro" (24).

So la María exists, she lives and she dies, but in others. María Cruz in the identity of la María exclaims, "No soy dueña de mi vida ni de mi muerte" (25), and later Maridalia tells her, "Tu vida no te pertenece, tu muerte no te pertenece" (29). The people need the life and death of others to manufacture their personal myths, even if those myths are destructive.

Maridalia, another of Josefa and Isabelita's acquaintances, leaves her husband to gain her freedom, but there is more than that, and the process encompasses another aspect of a kind of "religion of the mass media." At one point the characters receive news that a *yacaré* has escaped, and they rush to move aside a painting of "la última cena" (7), revealing a glass (*vidrio*) behind which the *yacaré* swims out in the world. What is this glass against the wall that shows the world? In the play it is the "Laguna de las Ilusiones"; it is also remarkably like a television set, and reminds one of its power in *La televisión enterrada*. After the *yacaré* takes her leg, Maridalia plunges into the *laguna*, retrieves it, and then becomes a devourer herself.

Traditional reality and traditional religion are replaced by a new reality and religion—the movies and television. They provide new objects to worship and which can be made into an alternate reality: Isabelita asks, "¿Por qué te gusta inventar tanto, hermana?" and Josefa answers, "Porque estoy viva, hermana" (22). People and things in the world can gain, lose, or change their reality since they can create and be recreated according to personal desire—Espinoza or Espinosa. Those who escape this symbiotic arrangement become devourers, like Maridalia. These are the only two choices. Those who choose to reinvent the world may expend less effort, but they remain trapped in a false or even nonexistent reality, as in *El teléfono* and *La televisión enterrada*. It is hard to say which is worse.

In the third stage of Espinosa's work, even the recreation is useless because his characters cannot change life. They can only become incorporated into it, since the bad that they may try to change cannot be changed at all. In *La noche de las nictálopes* an angel appears to the *hermanas Cordero* in a dream and sends them off on a silly, futile crusade to clean up a bar/brothel. It takes them most of the play just to arrive, and on the way a humorous catalogue of sins and sinners passes in review. It is a case of good versus evil, in which the latter is obvious but the former is not. One of the sisters' biggest battles occurs not against the sinful inhabitants of the town but against their own reactions. At times their first impulse is to combat the sin with violence (one sister wants to bring along an umbrella to "defend" themselves), and at others they have to struggle against the urge to join in the action and enjoy themselves. These two sisters are not the most fit agents for the angel's mission, as the angel should realize. But there are doubts about him, too. An old lady, whom he accuses of being a witch, is much more helpful to and supportive of the sisters, and she cautions them to beware of the angel "Luzbella." Although it is difficult to distinguish the good from the bad, it is clear that the bad triumphs in the end, if for no other reason than because the "good" (the sisters) gives up and goes home planning to try again another day.

Trying again will not help, though, as shown in *María o la sumisión*. This play criticizes the bureaucracy harshly, utilizing an approach similar to the fragmented style of Oscar Villegas. It is like watching a strobe light flash from gossipers to lazy workers to Don Juans to haughty bosses; it reveals abusive attitudes, ridiculous rules, jealousy, backbiting, and fighting. María, who arrives dressed in white, tries to remain pure, but it is futile because she becomes a part of what surrounds her. In one telling scene María engages in an argument with three mirrors, accusing them of being "burócratas" (53). They point out, quite rightly in this case, that, "La burócrata eres tú" (53). She may battle against bureaucracy, but she inevitably becomes a part of it because, as the *Licenciada* proudly proclaims, "¡La burocracia es eterna! Amen" (56). Good will lose to that eternal evil quite simply because good cannot win; it is too busy becoming the object of its struggle. There is no longer only one reality since it can be invented. Eventually, though, all the realities come to mirror each other, so much so that the time comes when it is no longer possible to distinguish one from the other, the good from the bad.

Sabina Berman and Tomás Espinosa depicted multiple realities. Berman asked what is real if people can create their own realities, as they do in "rewriting" history and in living their everyday lives. The multiple realities in the themes are emphasized by the multiple titles and texts that communicate them. Espinosa's answer to the question of what is real was that it does not matter, since everyone is that "reality," and it is everyone. Despite attempts to create better alternatives, people become *the* reality because they reflect it and it reflects them, because hypocrisy—two faces, the mirror—is the standard. Asking which is real and which is false is a waste of time. Because human beings are it, it simply reflects their "doubleness." In the end, then, no one should be surprised by Berman's multiple titles or by Espinoza/Espinosa's dual name. *All* of them are simultaneously the *real* title and the *real* name which, paradoxically, makes all of them less real. When identities become unstable, when history becomes clouded, after it becomes impossible to keep track of present-day reality, everything becomes real and everything becomes false in a world of many realities.

7. Spotlight on Society
Liera and Rascón Banda

Oscar Liera and Víctor Hugo Rascón Banda used theater to comment on society and its institutions. Liera grounded his plays on a broad base that includes literature, Mexican history and legend, and the idea that life and theater are equivalent. Rascón Banda built on an essentially realistic foundation and focused on the lower class in small towns, which is to say, not in Mexico City. If Sabina Berman questioned reality, Liera, at least at his most extreme, posited reality as theater: people are always creating and acting roles and cannot tell the masks from the reality because basically there is no difference. Rascón Banda, like Tomás Espinosa, viewed reality as a struggle between good and evil. While Espinosa seemed to hold out little or no hope for the triumph of good, Rascón Banda allowed at least a faint glimmer.

Oscar Liera

Liera was one of the most prolific writers of his generation. His plays are critical of government and church, and examine how Mexican history shaped both institutions. In an interview published in *Index on Censorship*, Liera talked about "demystifying Mexico": "This idea of demystification occupies my attention from several points of view. I'm concerned not only with our religion and our mystification of the pre-Hispanic past and the Revolution, but also with the myths that the world outside has created about Mexico" (37). These are the myths that have created Mexico's reality, those accepted and endorsed by social institutions to encourage the population's unthinking acceptance of Mexico's condition. If people simply accept, they stop thinking and give up their power to the institutions that shape their lives. Government is one of these institutions; the church is another, and the latter receives a large share of Liera's criticism. His plays suggest that the creation and perpetuation of church rituals— that is, myths—are theatrical: the creation of an alternate reality that demands from the spectator a willing suspension of disbelief, a giving up of one's reason. This is done by the theater, the church, the government, and eventually the people, so that in the end life comes to be ruled by rituals (myths), by the creation of roles, and by people playing at being people and even playing at playing.

The link between life and theater can be seen in many of the titles of Liera's plays: *Gente de teatro, gente horrible, Los fantasmas de la realidad* and *Las fábulas perversas* (two very different versions of a similar idea), and *La pesadilla de una noche de verano*. He also made frequent use of plays within plays and of myths based on many sources, such as the book of etiquette that rules the lives of the women in *Las juramentaciones*. *Inventario de indulgencias* involves an initiation into a fraternity or cult, and the trials of initiation resemble distorted religious practices, thereby suggesting that anything can be a religion and that such practices carry with them the possibility (or perhaps the probability) of fanaticism—of doing without thinking.

Liera presented his demythification and social commentary in a variety of forms. Some plays proceed in a linear fashion; others come in fragments that may be completely out of chronological order, such as in *El camino rojo a Sabaiba*, or arbitrarily rearrangeable by the director, as is the case of *La ñonga*. The subject matter ranges from scenes of contemporary life to Mexican history, legends, and other works of literature. *El Lazarillo* follows the *Lazarillo de Tormes* textually; *Las juramentaciones* shows shades of *La casa de Bernarda Alba*; *El camino rojo a Sabaiba* recalls *Pedro Páramo*; *Bajo el silencio* and *Un misterioso pacto* are linked by a common character reminiscent of El Merluza in Egon Wolff's *Flores de papel*; the title of *La pesadilla de una noche de verano* is an obvious reference to Shakespeare's play; *Los fantasmas de la reali-*

dad features a character whose exploits are similar to those of the legendary Fray Servando Teresa de Mier. As the vegetarians in *La piña y la manzana* (from the collection of the same title) talk about proper eating habits, one of them says, "No se debe comer nunca, una piña, junto con una manzana" (81). Liera's theater does not follow that kind of advice; it constantly mixes elements that should not be mixed and at times almost forces them upon the reader or spectator.

A complete commentary on such a diverse panorama would require a lengthy chapter just to itself. The focus here is on just three of Liera's plays, which still provide examples of his range, themes, and methods of communicating the themes. *Las Ubárry* includes one of his central themes, the creation of roles. *El jinete de la divina providencia* places a legendary character from Culiacán in concentric stage settings, time frames, and character groupings, thus providing an example of subject matter and structure. *Cúcara y Mácara* represents what Liera attempted to do most: to erase the lines between life and theater, between reality and fiction. In *Cúcara y Mácara* he did that, literally.

The mother and daughter in *Las Ubárry* are the last members of the Ubárry line, and to them falls the responsibility of ensuring the continuation of this, to their mind, very important family. Unfortunately, the daughter had to have an operation and one of its results was her inability to have children. This leaves that task to the sixty-two-year-old mother. To accomplish their goal, she must attract a man on one of their promenades around the park, and the action of the play consists of the preparations for that task. In a reversal of roles that continues throughout the play, the daughter makes up and chooses the clothes her mother will wear when she goes out to find a father for the required child. The stage directions explain, "La madre ha dejado su rostro en manos de su única hija para que lo cambie; y como si la muchacha también tratara de cambiar algo en el interior de la madre, habla" (55).[1] The daughter is literally creating a mask and another personality for her mother: a role in a play that requires certain dialogue and actions by the mother, and certain responses by the men who are also characters in this drama. After three months no suitable partner has been found and the mother recognizes the futility of the enterprise. However, the daughter is in control and can demand that at least the mother, if not the men, follow her direction.

As the previous quote indicates, the daughter is well aware of the importance of words in the creation of theater, but she insists on ignoring the silence to which the play constantly refers. Silence continually intrudes on the conversations between mother and daughter. It is compounded by the lack of any reaction by the men in the park, who obviously prefer the daughter and simply ignore the mother. The final stage direction makes clear the hopelessness of their situation: "Todo es en silencio, silencio como la condena a la que han sido entregadas" (64), a silence that includes the most important one of all, that of the daughter's body; the silence that assures the end of the family, despite the play that the two characters frantically write every day.

The danger to people's individual plays is silence or nonacceptance. At one point the mother cries, "¡No saldré a hacer el ridículo! No saldré, los hombres se ríen de mí. Se ve claro que es a ti a quien ellos prefieren" (63), but she is too weak to stand her ground, and the daughter talks her into continuing in her assigned role. Even though these two characters do not succeed with their drama, that does not mean that it is impossible for some people to create their own world and persuade others to inhabit it. *El jinete de la divina providencia* provides a good example.

El jinete is based on the legend of Malverde. In the play he is a Robin Hood-like character from before the turn of the century, about whose "miracles" present-day townspeople testify in order to sanctify him. The second- and third-hand accounts of the miracles pull speakers, listeners, audience, and reader into a circle of shifting reality and fantasy where time and the cause-effect relationship collapse. There are two concentric physical spaces onstage and two time frames: the exterior "present" narrates the interior "past." Malverde's story comes in pieces, according to whomever is testifying. The testimony simultaneously establishes facts and creates doubts about them. In Barthes's terminology, the play intertwines the proairetic and hermeneutic codes and the hermeneutic works to undermine the proairetic. The story recounts Malverde's exploits, but the principle enigmas of the hermeneutic code question precisely what he did or did not do (proairetic code). It is a play about how historical events are handed down, how reality is created, and who does the creating.

The actions in the play are presented out of chronological order and some of them are repeated. The effect is the creation of simultaneity at various points. In the present time space, people from primarily the lower class tell their second-hand stories to doubting representatives of the clergy. The stories concern Malverde, of course, but he never appears physically in either the present or the past spaces. He is a presence who, among the characters of the interior space, receives praise from the poor and creates fear and anger in the rich. The characters tell tales of Malverde's exploits, of the miracles after his death, of the rich Cañedo's attempt to frame him, and of various examples of the rich mistreating and even murdering the poor with impunity. All of these threads provide a clear comment on reality and the social establishments (government, church, and the rich-poor economic separation).

In the past time space those in control—the rich—make Malverde's existence possible by their corruption, but the "witnesses" in present time stress again and again that conditions have not changed. "Yo creo que, venerar a Malverde es como una forma de desafiar a los malos gobernantes" (VI); "Mi abuela . . . decía que el gobernador era un sinvergüenza, bueno las cosas no han cambiado mucho" (X); "Quiero decirle que en nuestro país las instituciones no funcionan, son un asco, están corrompidas" (XVII). The church does not fare any better than the government: "Malverde siempre ayudó a los pobres, estuvo al lado de ellos; aquí, el obispo sólo va a desayunar a la casa de los ricos" (VI). One of the early scenes portrays a religious procession (carrying a statue of the Virgin) that comes upon Martín in the process of raping the half-crazy Cuanina. The stage directions indicate: "La gente se burla, se ríe, los hombres por ver, y por descuido dejan caer a la virgen, la cual se hace mil pedazos" (VIII). This symbolic destruction is pointed enough, but it is compounded when the scene is repeated later in the play. The second time Cañedo, not Martín, is forcing himself on

Cuanina, but he immediately promises gifts to all those in the procession and explains to the priest that he had been intending to see about beginning construction of a new cathedral for the town. The priest then informs everyone present, "Esto es como un secreto de confesión, si alguien llega a revelarlo y lo comenta, queda excomulgado ipso facto; ahora que si no aguantan el gusanito y quieren decir por qué se nos rompió la virgen, diremos que fue Martín" (XVIII). This lie produced the first version of the scene, the town's "real" reality.

The hypocrisy and corruption of government and church form part of a larger pattern of realities that almost always are untrue. Martín saves Cuanina from abuse by several men, only to transform himself from defender into attacker and then from Martín to Cañedo, who is effectively transformed back into Martín by the priest. At another point Martín kills one of two workers who demand their pay, then accuses the other of committing the murder, knowing full well that the police will accept his (Martín's) account of the events.

The play's progress can be traced with Barthes's codes. The referential code encompasses the social aspect. The symbolic code includes the interior and exterior spaces, the destruction of the statue, and the use of recurring images such as stones and water. The semic code organizes the characters into two groups, rich and poor, while Malverde's history and the reaction of the rich (especially Cañedo) form the proairetic code. Finally, the reason for the stories—did Malverde really perform miracles that would qualify him for sainthood?—provides the hermeneutic element. With the addition of doubts about what happened and what is "real," a kind of super-hermeneutic code appears and undermines whatever faith the audience or readers might have had in the telling of Malverde's history.

The "super code" casts doubt on the form of Malverde's existence. In one instance he steals gold coins to distribute to the poor. Naturally anyone spending such coins can be arrested for complicity; by the evening of the following day, though, everyone in town has been arrested and freed, since the authorities cannot jail the entire population. One night Malverde receives a gunshot wound to his wrist, so the question of Malverde's identity will be clarified when the authorities find the person with a wrist wound. Unfortunately for the officials, by the next day everyone in town somehow seems to have injured and bandaged his or her wrist. Similarly, on another occasion everyone spends the day limping. "¿Coincidencia o milagro?" (XI) asks one of the witnesses. Or collusion? The townspeople may simply be protecting their champion, but another possibility also arises. Cañedo suggests, "Hay varios Malverdes" (XII); one of the priests interviewing witnesses laments, "Hasta el momento ni siquiera puedo precisar si Malverde existió o es un producto de las circunstancias sociales" (XIX), while another concludes, "Yo creo que en esa época todos eran Malverde" (XIX). Malverde may well not be one person, he may be the will or the conscience of the people. The explanation for his miracles lies in a comment by one of the priests: "Es que el pueblo, cuando quiere, hace milagros" (XIX). Therefore reality *can* be created.

El jinete de la divina providencia is a call for such a miracle. It is a comment on contemporary society, a challenge to change it, and an example of how change can be accomplished. The hope for change expressed in *El jinete* is not merely theatrical experimentation or antics; the hope for action by the spectators grows from a precedent created by Liera himself with *Cúcara y Mácara*, where he managed to move audiences to take theater and reality literally into their hands.

On 28 June 1981 *Cúcara y Mácara* was being performed at the Juan Ruiz de Alarcón theater in Mexico City. This play fiercely satirizes the clergy and the church on the basis of a plot that recalls the history of the Virgin of Guadalupe. Previous to June 28, this latter aspect in particular had provoked protests, and spectators had frequently shouted "Viva la Virgen de Guadalupe" during performances and followed with singing the "Himno Guadalupano" at the play's end. Uninformed members of the audience, assuming this extracurricular activity to be a part of the play itself, often joined in and gleefully shouted and sang along. Given these antecedents, then, no one was alarmed on the evening of 28 June when some thirty spectators rose from their seats in the first two rows and climbed onto the stage at the beginning of the second act. In fact, many accounts of the events that followed specifically mention the lack of any initial reaction: "El público asistente no daba crédito a lo que veía, ya que en un principio creyó que el ataque era parte de la obra" (Alfaro, 21). Those thirty spectators, however, then proceeded to take out pipes and sticks which they used to beat the director and the members of the cast for several minutes before fleeing the theater, leaving behind the bloodied actors and the bewildered audience.[2] At that moment *Cúcara y Mácara* ceased to be merely an anti-clerical satire and began to undergo a series of transformations that have effectively hidden the play's original identity.

The starting point for *Cúcara y Mácara* is a pair of episodes related to the legend of the Virgin of Guadalupe. The first is the well-known appearance of the Virgin to Juan Diego during Mexico's colonial period. Among the miracles she is said to have performed, the most significant is the reproduction of her own image on Juan Diego's shawl.[3] Liera's version is similar in that, many years before the action of the play, the Virgin of Siquitibum appeared before two orphans, Cúcara and Mácara, and her image was also preserved on a shawl. It should be mentioned that "siquitibum" forms part of a cheer, such as those used at athletic events, and that "cúcara, mácara" is the beginning of a children's rhyme, similar to "one potato, two potato" in English. This wordplay contributes to the play's humorous tone and at the same time begins to undermine the value of the word from the outset. These doubts as to the validity of words become central to the unfolding of *Cúcara y Mácara*.

The play's second historical antecedent is a lesser-known and more recent occurrence. According to Aquiles P. Moctezuma: "Un fanático colocó el 14 de noviembre de 1921 una espantosa bomba a los pies de la venerada imagen de Santa María de Guadalupe, fingiendo colocar un gran ramo de flores. La bomba estalló produciendo grandes desperfectos en el altar, pero respetando milagrosamente la imagen, de la cual no se rompió ni el cristal que la cubre" (282).[4] *Cúcara y Mácara* begins with a reference to an action similar to that of the explosion. In this case, immediately before the action of the play begins, an explosion completely destroys the image of the Virgin of Siquitibum. Fearing the consequences if the townspeople should discover that the image no longer exists, five priests use the day's alms to buy the silence of the police on the scene and frantically attempt to contact their superiors, the Bishop and the Cardinal. The Bishop finally arrives "con unas copitas, sin estar ebrio; digamos que viene alegre" (Liera 103).[5] The Cardinal's initial appearance is much more dramatic. He rushes in, steadies himself on a table as if he were about to faint, and proclaims, "Hermanos, hemos caído en un trance muy doloroso, nuestra santísima madre de Siqui nos ha abandonado . . . ¡¿Qué mano asesina e impía tuvo el atrevimiento de cometer tan sacrílego atentado?! ¡¡¿Dónde estaba yo cuando se cometió tan nefario acto?!!" (104). At that point one of the priests enters the room and innocently answers, "Estaba usted su eminencia, en otra fiesta, en casa de los Balderrama; aunque según su secretario usted había ido a visitar enfermos . . . " (104). After an uncomfortable silence the Cardinal regains his composure, reconstructs his fallen image, and the group looks for a way to hush up the disaster.

Unfortunately, several obstacles complicate their task. The Cardinal and the Bishop engage in a continuing conflict and frequently resort to name calling. "Womanizer" and "misogynist" are their favorites, and both terms seem to be appropriate and applicable. As this action occurs on stage, two nuns, invited by the Bishop and then refused admission by the Cardinal, continually knock on the door (offstage; they never appear) and ask, in vain, to be allowed to participate in the decision-making process. During this activity one of the priests insists on advancing his personal solution to the problem at hand. He claims that clergy and lay members alike should take advantage of this opportunity to eliminate their "learned faith"—the faith that they learn to have, but do not really feel (the myth mentioned by Liera in the interview)—and replace it with true faith. "¡Perdamos la fe todos!" he cries. "¡Destruyamos la idea de hacer los actos por costumbre! . . . Eso, que aprovechemos esta ocasión que nos brinda la divina providencia para que dejemos el culto a las vírgenes y nos volvamos hacia el espíritu santo" (107).

The mixture of all of these inharmonious voices results, of course, in utter confusion. The situation deteriorates so much that the group is, ironically, reduced to prayer, but as they begin a paper drifts down from above. Miraculously, it gives them a solution to their dilemma: replace the destroyed shawl, image, and frame with an exact copy on display in another church. They need simply erase the artist's signature on the copy and they will have created their own miracle—an explosion that damaged the altar but did no harm to the image of the Virgin. As an added bonus they can also proclaim sainthood for the friar who witnessed the explosion, thereby manufacturing their very own saint at the same time. As it turns out, the source of this miraculous solution is none other than the two nuns, who had to drop the paper from the rafters since the Cardinal would not allow them through the door. One of the priests even suggests that they conserve the paper as a religious relic. The play ends with everyone dancing around, shouting "¡Milagro!, ¡milagro!" (119) like people possessed, and singing a song in praise of their new saint, Saint Elgarberto.

The central element in the priests' search for a solution is the importance and power of the word. The priests must decide what to tell their parishioners to allow the latter to maintain their faith. Paradoxically, the first step in establishing the power of the word is the silence that must be imposed. No one, not even the police, can be permitted to know that the image was destroyed. Early in the play one of the priests declares that, "Esta noticia no puede trascender" (102), and later the Bishop explains, "Hemos decidido que nadie más debe enterarse de este hecho tan ignominioso que llena de vergüenza a nuestra grey, hasta que hayamos encontrado la solución" (114). The solution must involve a reconstruction of the broken fachada, the same kind of reconstruction that was forced on the Cardinal during his melodramatic entrance. No one can know that the paper bearing the solution exists, of course, for then the true nature of the "miracle" would be revealed. The priests must conceal the *real* truth and substitute *their* truth, which will then become *the* truth. Similar to the lie invented by the priest in *El jinete*, this type of substitution, forms the basis for the clergy's power in *Cúcara y Mácara*.

Liera's drama might well have gone unnoticed, but unlike most plays, *Cúcara y Mácara* can boast a whole series of "pseudodramatists" whose contributions have multiplied the play's original face many times over. One way to explain this evolution is with the structuralist concepts of "referent" and "signified." If "referent" is defined as the original or "real" object or event upon which a given discourse focuses—in this case the play itself—and if "signified" is the form in which one receives or understand the referent, then *Cúcara y Mácara* is a case of a single referent being subverted to such an extent that it results in at least four distinct signifieds. In other words, there are four different documents seen in the one original text that is the play. Following the process further, the referent itself, in combination with its subversions, leads to the creation of "secondary referents," other works that arise from and then mask the play as it existed in its initial form. In essence the play appears to be so many different things to so many people that the original version has been swallowed by its sub-versions.

This subversive process can be illustrated by referring to a diagram that represents the communication process. At the center is Ferdinand de Saussure's "signifier," an intermediate term that represents or takes the place of the original "true object" to which it refers. The "true object" is the "referent." The communicative act is possible because a sender and a receiver accept that the signifier is simply a convenient way to transform the referent into a form that may be expressed to the receiver. The signifier is, in fact, a "false" representation of a "true" object, just as the sound "tree" stands in the place of the green object growing in a field. Schematically the process takes this form:

$$referent$$
$$|$$
$$sender-----signifier----->receiver$$

The sender transforms the referent into a signifier to communicate it (the referent) indirectly to the receiver.[6]

Applying this scheme to the more concrete example of *Cúcara y Mácara*, it can be seen that the priests use their words to convey religious beliefs, feelings, and ideas to their congregation:

$$religion$$
$$|$$
$$priests-----words----->congregation$$

Extending this process of the substitution of a signifier for a referent, true faith finds its expression visually in images and saints, and even God is represented by intermediaries, the clergy. The result is a list of referents ("true objects") and their corresponding signifiers ("false representations"): religion and the word, faith and images, God and the clergy. The priest who suggests that everyone eliminate his or her "learned faith" and return to true faith is actually suggesting the elimination of the intermediate step—the signifier—so that he, as receiver, may communicate directly with God and experience true faith. In fact his explanation follows precisely that logic: "Pero ¿necesitamos intermediarios para hablar con nuestro Padre? ¡Pregunto! Hablemos con el pueblo y expliquemos lo sucedido. Llevemos a todos los fieles directamente al Señor, al espíritu santo . . . " (107).

Such a direct approach is distasteful for the other priests, to say the least, because it would result in the loss of their privileged position, which allows them to stand in place of true religion, faith, and God. They dare not risk the discovery by the congregation that a truth exists beyond what the priests represent. Over the years they have managed to substitute their truth, a "false representation," for the "real" truth. Religion in *Cúcara y Mácara* has become what the priests say it is; faith is not felt but seen in visual representations; and perhaps most importantly, the power and perfection of God are now attributed to the priests. Falseness has become truth, and the signifiers no longer communicate truth but *are* the "truth." Yet to maintain and exploit the power of their words, the priests must silence them. They must erase the signature on the substitute image—"Lo más sencillo será borrar esa firma" (116)—and destroy the paper—"Ese papel no puede guardarse como reliquia" (117). They cannot allow the members of their congregation the privilege of questioning the validity and the necessity of the signifiers (which include the priests themselves) or of realizing that the signifiers are transitory, that something more "substantial" and permanent may exist beyond them.

Cúcara y Mácara criticizes the clergy for occupying just such a position, for exaggerating its own importance, and for presuming to appear to be more than what it is in reality. In that sense the play criticizes the priests for taking advantage of the appearances that they are in a position to create. Liera seems to be suggesting that people must look beyond appearances and try to discover the real truth. Unfortunately the play produced just the opposite reaction.

From the beginning many people interpreted *Cúcara y Mácara* as an attack on religion, the Virgin of Guadalupe (referents), the clergy, and the church instead of just a criticism of the clergy and the church (signifiers). The protests began during the first performances in Xalapa with allegations that the play was "ofensiva e irrespetuosa con los sentimientos patrios y religiosos del pueblo mexicano" (D'Aquino Rosas), and culminated in the violence of 28 June in Mexico City. The protesters acted because they saw an attack on the clergy also as an attack on God and the Virgin. To a certain extent, then, they considered the clergy to occupy the same position as God, Virgin, faith, and religion. As a result the protests tended to prove the criticism expressed by the drama. Far from discrediting the play, the protesters' actions actually substantiated its theme. While they may have appeared to be doing one thing, they were actually doing quite another.

The protesters were the first to transform (subvert) *Cúcara y Mácara*. Their shouting and singing during the performances added a new element to the play which conveyed an additional message to its receivers. Thus, from the point of view of those who unwittingly sang and shouted along with the protesters, the play contains an additional signifier not present in the original work: an invitation to audience participation. The physical attack on the actors, the second signifier, also elicited a response, the third transformation, this time from the general public in the form of numerous articles expressing outrage at the attack on artistic freedom. The loss of artistic freedom became yet another signified, the modified message that *Cúcara y Mácara* represented to a wide range of artists, actors, directors, professors, students, and other groups. The next modification came with the dozens of articles published in the several days following the attack. All of them expressed basically the same ideas, even though each writer was careful to try to add his or her own original, personal touch. The result of this veritable avalanche of articles (signifiers) was essentially a self-contained body of literature, a sort of bastard son of *Cúcara y Mácara* that tells the same story from a truly astonishing number of viewpoints, none of which says anything about the play itself.

The original referent then, with the addition of its subversions, may signify any or all of the following: criticism of the clergy, attack on the Virgin, invitation to an audience sing along, or attack on artistic freedom. This broad and far from homogeneous range of signifieds resulted because successive receivers became senders or, in essence, supplementary authors. The first author, of course, was history as recorded in Liera's source material. Liera interpreted the historical events from his position as second-level author and produced *Cúcara y Mácara* in its original version. The sub-versions sprang from the protesters who sang and shouted (third-level authors), the ruffians who attacked the actors (fourth-level authors), the creators of a secondary literature (fifth-level), and then, of course, literary critics (sixth-level authors) who reduced the play and the events surrounding it to charts and structuralist terminology in order to produce papers and books, which form a tertiary literature.

Interestingly enough, the play in a sense anticipated these machinations. All of the subsequent "authors" of *Cúcara y Mácara* acted on the basis of their perception of the work—on appearance, which forms a part of the play's central thematic material. The Cardinal, the Bishop, the nuns, and the priests in the play make their decisions on the basis of appearances: what should the people see? How should the event appear to have happened? The visible surface (the signifier) becomes more important than the essence hidden behind it (the referent). What people see determines what they believe.

Cúcara y Mácara brings together a large number of the elements common to Liera's work—Mexican history, legend, society, and institutions, the satiric tone, and the social concerns—and makes them real. The comments here only touch the surface of his range, but they indicate his interest in the creation and debunking of myth, his concern with the state of the society that surrounds him, and his search for effective ways to communicate the need for change and to bring about some action outside the confines of the theater. Since the events surrounding *Cúcara y Mácara*, he continued to search for new and innovative ways to demystify Mexico and became one of the most prolific and interesting writers of the new generation.

Víctor Hugo Rascón Banda

Víctor Hugo Rascón Banda's work shows his commitment to social commentary. Although his plays are basically realistic in their language, characters, and settings, the plot develops in fragments that appear and accumulate due more to fate than to dramatic justification. There seems to be little control or reason behind many of the events, as in the case of *La fiera del Ajusco*. In this play, a series of the worst events society has to offer befalls Elvira, the poor, younger sister who follows her married sister to Mexico City. Elvira immediately has a child whose father runs away, continually loses jobs, has more children, and is detested by the mother of the man she finally marries (he cannot keep a job either). Despite her best intentions, she reaches the point where no one will lend her more money and she eventually kills her children, tries to commit suicide, and ends up in the hands of the police, where she is sentenced to forty years in prison. The play offers no dramatic explanation for most of these events. To an extent, that seems to be precisely the point in a world that is divided into black and white, bad and good, poor and rich. Good seems almost doomed, as in *Manos arriba*, where a pathetic jumble of characters looks for the easiest way to get their hands on money. Much like in the case of *La fiera del Ajusco*, in *Manos arriba* there is no love or emotion, only materialistic desires in this atmosphere where even the potentially good go bad. This is the fate of those at the bottom of the heap, and there seem to be only two ways to escape this fate—revolution or divine intervention, and neither of those is sure.

The lower class suffers more than its share of violence in Rascón Banda's early plays. *Los ilegales* depicts the realistic life of Mexicans who cross illegally into the United States. The play's realism derives from its language, characters, and the conditions that surround them, and is underscored by introducing each scene with quotes from newspapers and magazines. The quotes describe events and provide information about actual cases. The first act shows a variety of miserable conditions families experience in Mexico, thus establishing reasons for wanting to cross the border. Act II provides a litany of terrible situations in the United States: *coyotes* who take advantage of those they bring across the border, greedy yankee bosses, hindrance from fellow illegals, and even a meeting of the Ku Klux Klan. This view of those who cross the border illegally focuses on the worst possible conditions, and its effect is to provide historical information more than a dramatic experience.

The sweeping violence seen in the lives of the groups designated as *ilegales* is focused on individuals in *Las armas blancas*. This series of short plays resembles the early works of Gerardo Velásquez. They grow around a central mystery that is never revealed completely. The *armas blancas*—a machete, a knife, a letter opener, and a dagger—function as phallic symbols, and the plays have undercurrents of sexual control, *machismo*, homosexuality, and undefined past relations. The importance of these currents remains unclear, but they inevitably lead to murder: of a father by his son, of a brother and sister by their mother, and of innocents by those looking for vengeance.

The violence moves toward the suggestion of revolution in the historical *Tina Modotti* and becomes part of the action in *Voces en el umbral* and *El baile de los montañeses*. *Tina Modotti* is composed of twenty-eight fragments that trace the life of the model-photographer-revolutionary. The action simply chronicles her adventures; the revolutionary aspect is reflected in the experimental structure. In the written text the fragments appear chronologically, but Rascón Banda also lists two alternate sequences before the play's text: one based on thematic oppositions and one based on parallels among three periods in Modotti's life.

Voces en el umbral, which also has a historical setting, follows a family as it travels from Spain to Mexico to work in the mines. Its basic theme concerns the racism inherent in the treatment of the Indians who work the mines and act as servants to their non-Indian bosses and companions to their children. The simple and direct story develops chronologically from the early memories of the Spanish daughter in the family and ends with her "overthrow" by her Indian companion since childhood. The play, which can serve as a metaphor for Mexican history, avoids moralizing with its lyrical, stylized language. This basic, straight-forward play, Rascón Banda's second, sets the tone for much of the rest of his production.

The dance in *El baile de los montañeses* serves as a metaphor in a village where everyone must dance to the tune of the government and cannot stop once their dance of death has begun. Again the story follows a simple, chronological development based on a good-bad division explained by one of the characters: "Las cosas no nacen ni se hacen solas. Siempre hay un par. Blanco y negro, bien y mal, noche y día. Para toda hierba mala, existe la contra hierba" (38). The *hierba mala* consists of the corrupt officials who plan the dance and the soldiers who force the townspeople to dance. These bad elements abuse the good, which include the honest official, the citizens, and even the rebels, who are not so much sympathetic as merely justified in their actions. The abuses and tensions increase until the only recourse left the townspeople is defection to the rebel side.

Characterization in the play is less important than the movement of the story, in which things just happen. The importance of the idea of lack of control is made clear in the first scene, where several men taunt the retarded Beto until he suffers an epileptic seizure, and again when the soldiers force the people to dance at gunpoint. Don Lalo spells out one way for the people to regain control of their lives: "Yo recuerdo que antes de la Revolución, así empezaron las cosas . . . Con descontento. Con gente que se iba desesperada a esconderse a la sierra y desde allá se levantaba" (73). That is one solution. In *La maestra Teresa* Rascón Banda suggests another: a miracle.

The action in this play occurs in two dramatic spaces and seems to move along two separate temporal lines. In the past Santa Teresa de Jesús writes and counsels two young novitiates. In the present the *directora* of a private school consults with an *Inspector Escolar* and a representative of the teachers' union about removing *la maestra* Teresa, who has not shown up to teach for a week. While the play seems to describe two separate events at the beginning, the line between them quickly begins to blur. Juan, a mildly retarded custodian at the school whom the *directora* blames for all her problems, is similar to an inhabitant of the convent whom Santa Teresa scolds for entering her cell while wearing his shoes. There are also similarities between the two novitiates and Juan's retarded twin daughters, who live at the school with him. Finally, both spaces are similar in their rigidity. The rigidly religious Santa Teresa counsels the two novitiates on the importance of spirituality over such "trivial" matters as eating and sleeping, and the *directora* insists on rigidly traditional schooling where the students, all female, learn to memorize and not to think (and even to not think). *La maestra* Teresa is a problem not only because she has stopped giving classes, but because she had begun to introduce new (and unacceptable to the *directora*) teaching methods and materials, including *poesía mística*.

The two plot lines first alternate and then converge when it is discovered that *la maestra* Teresa has become Santa Teresa. She tells the Inspector, "Teresa Sánchez de Cepeda y Ahumada no existe ya. Ahora sólo soy Teresa de Jesús, indigna sierva de Vuestra Merced" (52). She also reveals certain interesting information about the *directora* that establishes her corrupt administration of the school's business and her amorous adventures.

Teresa's mental state is not clarified at the end. Her transformation into the saint would appear not to be possible but for two occurrences. First, the life-sized figure of the crucified Christ on the wall of her cell comes to life in scenes when she is alone and in the last scene leaves hand in hand with her. Second, Juan and his two daughters are retarded and stammer or are mute in the presence of the *directora*, but are perfectly normal in the presence of Teresa. The explanations for these events are left to the spectator. What is suggested, however, is that it will take some sort of miracle to clean up the educational system, the play's fundamental point.

The doubts about what is real that form a part of *La maestra Teresa* appear again in *Playa azul*. Family members reunite at a run-down beach hotel where the father has called them together in hopes of saving the hotel. The present-time action, however, operates completely at the mercy of a past shrouded in secrets and mystery, at least for the audience. The family is haunted by ghosts: the father's illegal activities, the mother's past as a prostitute, the son's kidnapping and subsequent stay in a "clinic," and the daughter's hatred for her brother. All of this is merely suggested in the dialogue, so the audience can only guess at the characters' antecedents. The play shows a trail of wreckage: the lives of the characters, the division of the family, and the hotel itself, which was damaged by an earthquake. In this context the father's political activities and enemies and the family's social standing become metaphors for yet another level of wreckage— Mexico itself, suffering under the weight of corruption and doubts about the past that has produced its present. This is yet another expression of one of the primary concerns of this generation of dramatists.

Rascón Banda returns to the black and white division of characters and to divine hope with *Máscara vs. Cabellera*. The play's action revolves around the world of professional wrestling, and Apolo García in particular. He is a thirty-year-old wrestler who begins with the intention of cleaning up the wrestlers' union and then evolves into a Christ figure. He is pure; he insists to his girlfriend that they will enjoy each other only spiritually. "Por mi compañía, nada más" (221), he tells her. He is betrayed by his best friend, and then apparently dies in the ring in a titanic match against his betrayer. When his mother and girlfriend go to claim the body, however, it is nowhere to be found. He seems not to have died after all, so he is out there somewhere, obviously still struggling to make the world a better place. His mother says, "Aparecerá como Apolo II. Vamos a la arena. Apolo vive" (251).

Where Tomás Espinosa found almost no hope for changing his black and white dramatic world, Víctor Hugo Rascón Banda found at least some, however faint and contradictory: revolution or divine intervention—along the lines of Oscar Liera's *divina providencia*, perhaps. By any account, they all viewed society as plagued by nearly insoluble problems, and in this they coincided with almost all of the other writers of their generation (both in and out of Mexico). The real differences came with their presentation of that view. Liera's characters seek to reinvent reality in their own image, and according to their own script. With everyone involved in that same project, the chances are that they will succeed from time to time: "Es que el pueblo, cuando quiere, hace milagros" (*El jinete*, XIX). Rascón Banda found fewer miracles because he dug deep into common, everyday reality, where his characters have little opportunity to invent their own fate because they are so busy battling against it. The triumphs in both cases are few and far between, but Liera's characters amuse themselves by believing they can create them, and by refusing to see the defeats. Rascón Banda's characters suffer under their defeats, and most times must content themselves only with being able to survive.

8. Bridging the Gap
The Second Wave

As has been noted, the second wave of Mexico's new drama brought with it an explosion of playwrights, plays, publications, stagings, workshops, and general interest. The renewed enthusiasm began in 1979, and over the next several years a continuing series of events kept young dramatists in the public eye. This produced more possibilities for staging and publishing works, more attention from the public and the theater establishment, and more publicity. Taken together, they made writing for the theater seem less futile than it had been for so many years, and large numbers of potential dramatists jumped at the chance for success.

A significant amount of credit for the revival of theater by young Mexican playwrights must go to the Universidad Autónoma Metropolitana and its "Nueva Dramaturgia" series. This effort, which dates from 1979, devoted itself to regularly scheduled readings and stagings, and then publication by the university, of plays written by young dramatists. It was perhaps the first time that anyone other than Emilio Carballido had made much effort toward helping this group of writers to succeed, and they took full advantage of the opportunities.

Also in 1979, Sabina Berman began a streak that drew attention to the quality of the work being produced by new playwrights. That year she won her first INBA *Premio Nacional de Teatro*, for *Bill*. The play was published and staged the next year, and in 1981 Berman won the *Premio Nacional* again, for *Rompecabezas*. In 1982 she won yet again, this time in the division for children's theater; in addition, *Rompecabezas* was published and *Bill* was republished in Carballido's popular *Más teatro joven*. One year later Berman won her fourth *Premio Nacional* for *Anatema (Herejía)* and *Bill* was staged again, followed by *Herejía* the next year. Her successes culminated in the publication of an anthology of her plays in 1985. This kind of success was almost unheard of, and naturally it attracted attention for both Berman and new Mexican theater.

The third important event of 1979 was Carballido's publication of a second edition of *Teatro joven de México*, which contained several of the plays from the ill-fated first version, plus a number of new ones. This time there was more interest and the collection sold well, going into several printings.

The notoriety surrounding the staging of Oscar Liera's *Cúcara y Mácara* came in 1981, and attracted not only attention but reaction from the public. By 1982 Carballido was ready with another volume of plays, *Más teatro joven*, which was even more popular than the collection published three years earlier.

During this time the UAM was constantly staging, publishing, and publicizing new plays, round tables were organized for the new dramatists, short plays appeared in Sunday newspaper supplements, and the Editores Mexicanos Unidos decided to devote an entire line to Mexican theater, with one branch of it reserved exclusively for young writers. That was the source of Berman's collection, which was preceded by one devoted to Oscar Villegas.

With so much going on in so many different arenas, it could not help but attract attention, and this attention fed the hopes of all the young dramatists who suddenly appeared. Given the length of the list, an organization into groups on the basis of some common characteristic is necessary. The eighteen dramatists presented here can be divided into four categories: four writers with a sustained production, four more whose work is associated primarily with the *Teatro joven* series, seven who worked mainly outside of Mexico City, and seven more who had less than four works available. It should also be mentioned that there were more dramatists writing than those included here; their work was simply unattainable either in published form or in personal manuscripts. As it is, many of the plays described here apparently exist only in manuscript form and were supplied by the authors or their friends, or were obtained from sources such as the collections of the *Sociedad General de Escritores Mexicanos* (SOGEM) or the *Centro de Investigaciones Teatrales Rodolfo Usigli* (CITRU).

Four with a Sustained Production

Antonio Argudín's plays range from the fantastic to the realistic. He wrote very short plays, often humorous, dealing with the theme of false hopes and with the contrast between love, nature, and art on the one hand, and money and civilization on the other. In *Cypris*, the gods Cypris and Eros arrive in New York City and attempt to turn Manhattan into a paradise. In the strictly realistic *Sueldo según capacidades*, a girl untrained for secretarial work applies for a secretarial position but has to settle for working as a prostitute instead, due to her lack of skills in the job of first choice. Argudín's dichotomy pits fantasy, such as the gods and the girl's hopes, against reality—Manhattan and the girl's abilities.

Alejandro Licona's first plays are humorous, but the humor is gradually supplanted by violence. In one early play, *El diablo en el jardín*, the devil tries to win Teofilo's soul, but Teofilo is too good to be bad and never manages to accomplish the evil act necessary to qualify him for hell.

Huélum o cómo pasar matemáticas sin problema shows how the educational system works. Instead of studying, three boys plan to buy good grades from a teacher, and two of them devote extraordinary efforts to obtaining the necessary money (illegally). They pay, but when the teacher fails to produce the expected grades, they accost him, and the police come and haul the boys away. The farcical humor turns darkly ironic when the boys-turned-men are interviewed years later and, despite their failure in school, one is a successful writer, one has become rich through inheritance and by owning crop land (one crop, mentioned casually, is marijuana), and the third is the President of the Republic. The play suggests that the educational system encourages cheating instead of learning, and that that is enough to produce a happy, good life—a presidential life, in fact.

Esta es su casa begins humorously, when a mother and her young daughter arrive from Veracruz and appear on the doorstep of another mother and daughter in Mexico City. The first pair had met the second two years earlier and now have come to live in the city. There is a problem, however, and they need a place to stay for a few days. The few days become a week, then two, then several. The unwanted visitors never lift a finger to help, and the visiting girl is loud, destructive, and thoroughly unlikeable. The apartment owners, on the other hand, grow more and more desperate since they cannot simply tell the visitors to leave. Instead they finally pretend they have to move in an attempt to free themselves. The humor gradually sinks under the growing tension and frustration.

With *Máquina* the humor fades entirely, and the criticism focuses on industry where, with the exception of a few workers, everyone involved in the system and the system itself are corrupt and bad. The play pits the unfeeling administrators against the mistreated workers and the workers against each other. All are set in a backdrop of sex, safety violations that result in injury and death, blackmail, strikes, rampant unfairness, and a situation in which almost everyone's sole concern is his or her own welfare. The resulting inhumanity is reflected in the title.

Licona's contribution to the wave of historical plays focuses on a group of Mexican martyrs, Los Niños Héroes. *El día de mañana* takes place in Chapultepec castle on 12 September 1847. The criticism is directed less toward the North American invaders than toward Mexico's leaders and their corruption that dooms the country to debt and defeat. At the end one of the Cadets says, in reference to those leaders, "Ellos no son el pueblo. Yo lucho por el pueblo. Por mí. Y así como de improviso todos nos juntamos para combatir al enemigo, el día de mañana lo podemos hacer para derrocarlos a ellos, a los verdaderos traidores . . . " (139). The present-day struggle between those in authority and the common people is thus extended over a hundred years into the past. It is a problem that, according to these plays, remains unresolved.

Licona's social criticism moved from humorous to violent, and from good versus bad to almost all bad. This nearly hopeless view has been seen in previous chapters, and Licona suggested why that hopelessness is more and more common. In *Huélum*, the television interviewer at the end explains, "En México no hay corrupción y eso se lo pueden preguntar a cualquier político, a cualquier maestro, a quien quieran" (299). The politicians are in charge of Mexico today, the teachers are in charge of those who will be in charge in the future, and they along with everyone else are so busy protecting themselves that they have no time or energy to intervene. In Licona's view, the self-serving attitudes and the insistence on self-preservation create the problem.

José López Arellano continued writing from the first *Teatro joven* through *Más teatro joven*. He published five plays, all very short and basically realistic pictures of life in the city. Realistic dialogue predominates over action, and the earliest works show a touch of humor. *El soplete*, for example, takes place on a bus. A drunk gets on, argues with the driver about the fare, then sits down beside a young man and begins to talk. The young man obviously wants nothing to do with him and barely responds, but the drunk insists on acting like an old friend with his incessant but seemingly sincere anecdotes, comments, questions, and laments about his travails. Anyone who has ever been trapped by one of these ubiquitous types can understand the young man's desperation and will not be surprised to find that the drunk ends by asking for and then demanding a handout. The situation depicts a common occurrence, as does *En el hueco de la mano*, in which two women on a street corner beg and converse. Ironically, the begging is almost incidental for them, since their real interest lies in their conversation. These are basically scenes from real life transferred to the stage.

Querido diario is a monologue in which a young man recreates a failed dinner with his date. The situation lends itself well to López Arellano's style because the young man talks and talks and merely reacts to the limited actions of the other "characters" (pausing while his date supposedly answers him and then responding to her, for example). He talks mainly about his frustrations, self-doubts, and sufferings, from a basis of borderline paranoia and a full-blown inferiority complex. In fact, the characters in all five plays deal with their problems by talking about them, and in four of the five cases all the words lead to dead ends because the characters are incapable of maintaining relationships with others. In the case of the beggars it is for social reasons, and in the case of the young people, it is their neuroses. The primary focus, then, falls on interaction (or the lack of it), between people.

Eusebio Ruvalcaba also emphasized the characters over the action and the themes, although his plays exhibit a touch of social consciousness. He wrote one-acts exclusively, most with surprise endings. *¡Ahí viene! ¡Ahí viene!* parodies the awful service one receives in government offices and the relative value of people in a hierarchy. An elderly woman trying to arrange her pension is soundly ignored and finally threatened and attacked by several thugs, who turn out to be secret service and body guards for the President, who is coming to visit the office that day. In *La visita* two thieves are preparing to leave for Acapulco with their loot, but one insists on visiting his grandmother's grave to say goodbye. As he talks to and about her, though, he decides that the best thing he can do with his share of the money is to build a church in her honor.

The *Teatro Joven* Connection

Four playwrights who published only one or two works appear in Carballido's *Teatro joven* collection. All four were concerned with social commentary, concentrating on the police, on medical services, and on *machismo*.

Casto Eugenio Cruz and Felipe Galván both focused on the police's brutal treatment of prisoners, and in both cases prisoners whose identity has been mistaken. In Cruz's *Taller de ciencias sociales* the police mistake the address, raid the wrong house, and brutalize the wrong person. The theme is police as buffoons, and violent buffoons at that. Galván's *La historia de Miguel* is more extensive and deals with the beginnings of a revolution in the countryside. It tells the story of how Miguel becomes what the Argentinians call a *desaparecido*. The first scene, filled with a tension reminiscent of that in Agustín Yáñez's *Al filo del agua*, focuses on Miguel's simple daily life in the small town where he runs a small store. It also establishes the apprehension created by the characters' feeling that something is about to happen.

They are right, for near the end of the scene the authorities come and arrest him because they are convinced he is a rebel. The rest of the play deals with his interrogation by police and with his wife's futile search for him as she is sent from jail to jail, always with the promise that in another prison she will find information on his whereabouts. Both plays use realistic language and straightforward, chronological presentations. The intensity of the criticism helps to establish the tension.

Silvia Marín's "buffoons" work in a hospital run by the *Seguro Social*. They symbolize a blind, uncaring bureaucracy at its worst, providing poor service and even mistreating emergency room patients to the extent that their suffering at times leads to death. The receptionist exempts herself from responsibility by repeating, "Este hospital tiene reglas, yo las cumplo" (397). That is her excuse for bad treatment of the patients, for not thinking, and for doing only the minimum—and doing that badly. The language is realistic and the characters are basically types, but the receptionist, the security guards, and the patients and their families acquire a very human aspect, since they all feel trapped against the blank, uncaring, inhuman wall of the bureaucracy. Their shared helplessness and frustration provide tension in the play and give it vitality.

Teresa Valenzuela provided a woman's view of *machismo*. *Estela y la geografía política* is a fairly standard depiction of students at a party, where their concerns revolve around drinking, sex, and not studying. Estela is rejected by one boy because she gets better grades, and seduced by another merely so she will help him improve his own grades. *Dijeron que a todos* is more interesting because of the extreme level of hypocrisy and irony. An unrepentently gross and pretentious *macho* type tells his friend stories of past conquests and advises him to come on to *all* girls in his vicinity. The friend takes the advice, but his first targets happen to be the sister and the girlfriend of his advisor, and the latter promptly defends them (physically), and then preaches to the pair about avoiding abusive *macho* types. The tone is steadfast and obvious about the girls' distaste for the boys' attitudes and the virtual impossibility of building a relationship around that kind of thinking. The play's tension derives from the strong characters and the irony that surrounds them.

Outside Mexico City

If it is difficult for playwrights to make a living or even gain attention for their work in Mexico City, the center for theater in Mexico, then in areas outside the capital the problems of publishing and staging are multiplied many times over. There is a smaller market for books, and their circulation and distribution are poorer. Staging presents bigger problems if for no other reason than the lack of theaters. During most of the period under consideration Guadalajara, Mexico's second largest city, had only two commercial theaters. Thus productions of new plays occurred mainly in out-of-the-way school or university theaters, with little or no accompanying publicity, and in amateur theater competitions where the audience members tended to be less interested in watching the play than in seeing their friends and relatives on stage.

Not surprisingly, the plays written by dramatists outside Mexico City do not deal primarily with realistic life in the city, as do so many of the works produced in the capital. They are also much more varied in form (relative to their number), sometimes approaching a line between what is commonly considered to be theater and some other artistic form. They do have in common an extremely critical view of society. Although there are undoubtedly many more writers, this sample covers those whose plays exist or have existed in published form.

Plays by Dolly S. de Velasco, Conrado Ulloa Cárdenas, and José Ruiz Mercado are offered in *3 piezas de teatro joven jalisciense*. Velasco's *La carretera a Tokaido* consists of a kind of *capa y espada* situation where everyone at an inn tries to deceive everyone else, and the result is a moral for the audience. In *Maldita inquisición* Ulloa Cárdenas criticized clerics in a series of episodes that present many examples of bad priests and only one of a good one.

Pshklmania, by Ruiz Mercado, expresses basically what its title does—a "nothing," a meaningless society where nothing matters. At various times the characters sing a song reminiscent of the chant of the three children in José Triana's *La noche de los asesinos*: "Lo bello no es lo bello, / como lo grande no es tan grande, / Todo esto es lo que tú piensas, / y lo contrario, irracional te parece" (101). The play takes the point of view of Marixa, a crazy girl who talks to chickens and a make-believe friend. The language, while never realistic, sometimes borders on the absurd, with relationships appearing impossible. What *is* possible is the creation of one's own reality, which for Marixa turns out to be a prison. Basically the action in the play is self-defeating and comes to nothing in the end, like the nothing that the title expresses.

Ruiz Mercado communicated the same ideas in a somewhat more accessible form in *Como cualquier historia de familia*. The play paints a society in disintegration. The *cualquier* of the title suggests the masses, nothing individual, and as such the humanity is squeezed out of the characters. The play is about a society where jobs involve mindless repetition, and where a man marries, has children, has affairs, and is arrested for no apparent reason. The wife is also interrogated and when she and her husband's lover meet (while trying to free him from prison) they both decide to abandon him since, "La inocencia también es culpable" (344). That kind of absurdist touch characterizes the dialogue at times. The characters are also aware that reality holds no particular importance. One of them says, "La ficción podemos hacerla nuestra, la verdad no" (330). Their primary truth consists of a life that runs in circles, where one day is like all other days and seems as much like death as life.

The play moves on the thin thread of a chronological plot, but what predominates is the occasional absurdist moment, the non-realistic language, the repetition (such as an early scene that repeats late in the play), and the anonymous people in generic situations. The play criticizes mechanical, empty life and the search for something meaningful as well as the police, who also involve themselves in a meaningless search for some unspecified meaning. In short, it presents a depressing picture of a society where nothing really matters, and in that sense it expresses the same theme as *Pshlkmania*. This empty reality is similar to the picture that appeared time after time in plays from the second wave.

Hiram Sánchez Félix's *El perfil del aire* also offers social protest, but with an optimistic solution. It shows the ideal president—one who takes care of the poor, in part by taking land from the rich and giving it to those who deserve it or legitimately own it. The president suffers from a degenerative disease that finally drives him crazy, so the hopes ostensibly expressed by the play turn out to parody themselves and lose their meaning, thus reflecting the case of the president, whose hallucinations slowly take the place of his reality.

The subtitles of two of Miguel González Gómez's plays are *Teatro poético* and *Teatro de Eros*. González Gómez wrote theater that is completely atypical from the usual sense of dramatic theater. His works have characters but no characterization, language that many times consists of lists that serve as images, and acts and scenes that do not contribute to dramatic structure or movement. His characters are designated with "names" such as Niño and Madre, but those indications are almost incidental, since the characters behind them are primarily outlets for the imagery.

The works tend to be very short; one is two pages long. As a result little time is available to create dramatic movement, a story-line, traditional conflict, or tension, even if those were intended. At times there is only a minimal movement of any kind, since the lists (each character speaks one or two words) can consist only of nouns. They provide a kind of visual and auditory experience that results in more of an atmosphere or feeling than a traditional dramatic experience. One would be hard pressed to produce them as drama; they could, however, be theatrical, consisting of perhaps music, dance, and light to help add meaning to the words. The words do convey a feeling that emphasizes nature, and they suggest its superiority over civilization. At times the effect borders on expressionism, and at other times the lists reflect surrealism's automatic writing. The dialogue is not really poetry either. As much as anything, the works seem to be experiments in creating a communal experience and in stretching the limits of what can be considered as "theater."

Félix Vargas, also from Guadalajara, wrote about the rebellion of the young but from the point of view of an older generation. He commented on the education of young people in terms of their elders' expectations, and directed a current of satire at the church. In *Jesús, María y José* the religious figures are placed in contemporary society, but the religious element tends to get in the way of the social criticism. *Las dos soledades* is about youthful rebellion, although the rebellion of the twins referred to by the title constitutes only a small part of the action.

Guillermo Schmidhuber de la Mora, based in Monterrey, wrote didactic plays built on the frame of a clever twist and experimentation with dramatic expression conveyed directly to the audience. The experiments included bringing reality to the theater, by taking reality and putting it, instead of drama, on the stage. He also used characters and narrators who speak directly to the public, repetition of scenes, and layering of actions. *Todos somos el Rey Lear* exhibits the piling of layer on layer. The "actors" are members of a real family who happen to be actors who have been presenting *King Lear*, but who, for the current performance (the play *Todos somos el Rey Lear*), are reenacting a real event connected to their staging of *Lear*. In *Todos somos el Rey Lear* a person in the same predicament as King Lear invites the actors in a production of *King Lear* to dinner. They are to reenact scenes so that the host can try to understand his own situation. *Todos somos el Rey Lear*, however, is merely a reenactment of what happened at the dinner, and the reenactment is interrupted by a member of the audience (an actor playing a real person). He claims that the action on stage is not a true representation of the dinner, but he is soon challenged by yet another audience member. This second "spectator" claims that the first is a fraud (an actor), thus establishing the "reality" of the second, who is really the person who gave the dinner. To confuse the issue even more, this whole series of events is revealed to have taken place several years before the action in the theater. It is not reality taking place before the audience's bewildered eyes after all. Rather, it is a representation of reality, so the *real* real person turns out to be false as well. The work's theme begins as the theme of *King Lear*, but the play of realities becomes so strong that a new theme—what is real—eventually overwhelms the original idea.

In *La catedral humana* one scene is repeated three times in different epochs, and the recycling of events in time suggests that people never learn from history. *Lacandonia*, about the present-day treatment of the Mayas, includes several alternative endings, each played out in its turn as the narrator/commentator calls it up, and all producing the same result. The lessons deal with the destruction of nature at the hands of civilization, seen in a dichotomy in which civilization equals the desire for money and power (bad), and nature equals the Indians and truth (good).

There is only minimal character development in these plays, since the characters serve primarily to communicate the central message. These lessons are summarized in monologues that at times are spoken directly to the audience. The development of relationships among the characters occupies a secondary level, and much of their interaction takes place offstage. The plays experiment with the use of theater to communicate lessons in life by becoming self-referring and by confusing the line between the fiction of the stage and the reality of the outside world. If the action played out is real and not fiction, then the audience will tend to pay closer attention, since their expectations of what a theatrical experience is will be upset.

Writers with One, Two, or Three Plays

This section focuses on seven playwrights whose works range from musicals and farce to strong criticism of corruption, primarily by the government.

For a time American musicals were popular in Mexico, but very few were written for the legitimate stage by Mexicans. Alejandro Aura, Claudio Patricio, and Agustín Bandrich all contributed a kind of cabaret play with music, songs, and, on occasion, dance. Aura's *Salón Calavera* is a club where the action between performances centers on *machismo* and corrupt unions. *Las visitas* begins as a parody of hospital care—a patient who refuses to tolerate any more visitors, preferring instead to spend his time with the two nurses who are his constant companions—and at the end becomes a statement on free will, when the patient chooses to die. *Bang . . . !* is a Wild West extravaganza complete with good guys, bad guys, Indians, Mexicans, shoot outs, pursuits, train robberies, and more. Humor predominates as the characters sing their way through their adventures.

Patricio's *Día de graduación* combines a theater-caberet atmosphere with concerns about the events of 1968. The comedy routines and the love of the theater's physician for the star contrast with the mental scars left on the doctor by his proximity to the violence surrounding Tlatelolco when he was a medical student. When the star is fired, he lets loose the violence he has apparently been suppressing over the years.

Bandrich's *El Condor Travesti* concerns the drug traffic associated with a traveling transvestite show, and expands to include the question of land reform and violent police tactics when the managers of the show are arrested and thrown in with other criminals. Bandrich's main target seems to be the police, a possibility underscored by his other play, *Réquiem para Lecumberri*, which deals specifically with conditions in that prison and soundly condemns them.

Dentro de estos ocho muros by Rafael Ramírez Heredia was published in the same anthology as *Réquiem para Lecumberri*. In Ramírez Heredia's play two series of actions alternate, although they are understood to be taking place simultaneously. In one, a pair of government officials plots the assassination of an important general, and in the other the lover of the wife of one of the officials convinces her that she must pump her husband for information. The concern in both series is deceit, although the play ends before they come together.

Both Leonardo Kosta and Eduardo Rodríguez Solís wrote farces based on modern myths. Kosta's *La pata de Santa Anna* supposes that the famous leg is found in the excavations in Mexico City, and the action follows the schemes to gain possession of the leg. The plots and counterplots intertwine the corrupt politician and his mistress, the greedy *gringo* who cannot speak correct Spanish, the voice of God who assures the politician that the leg is holy, and the revelation that the voice was actually the author of the play intent on exacting revenge on the politician. The play becomes anti-politicians, anti-Yankee, and ultimately anti-drama, with its Pirandello-inspired author who must trick his characters because he apparently cannot control them.

Rodríguez Solís's secret agents in *El encuentro de los agentes secretos* combine James Bond, Rudolph Valentino, Bella Otero, and Sarah Bernhard (as Bond Valentino and Bella Bernhard).[1] In addition there is a character referred to as Tercer Personaje who stands by onstage and offers comments and explanations. This last character makes the project clear from the outset: "Intrigas, porque todo está hecho de esta manera. Hoy tú, mañana nosotros. Hoy matas, mañana matamos. Y la sangre se derrama como el dinero sobre el planeta. Y las mujeres se entregan a los hombres. Y la vida rueda . . . " (8). The play parodies spy thrillers of the James Bond variety, which are almost parodies themselves. Valentino ransoms an important bureaucrat from the rebels, represented by Bernhard, who tries to seduce him into backing the "just" rebel cause instead of the "unjust" bureaucrats.

Margarita Díaz Mora also included a kidnapping and a backdrop of corruption in *La mariposa incorruptible*, but in a more realistic vein. A boy is determined to follow in the footsteps of his adored father, a judge. However, the boy is kidnapped and presented with evidence of years of the father's corruption. At the same time the price of the boy's freedom, made known to the father, the mother, and the grandmother, is a public admission by the father of his practices. The effect on the family creates the tension and provides character development as the family members attempt to accept the truth of the father's actions while he continues to deny and justify them.

These plays condemn the corruption in society and government, much like the works from the first wave of writers, but the focus on teenagers and their personal suffering is gone. Now, instead of seeing everything from the point of view of the young, the dramatists employed a number of perspectives, including that of the corrupt parties themselves. The styles and forms are more varied, and the variety allows for much more experimentation to break out of standard dramatic form. The plays exhibit a more liberal use of fantasy, more stylization of presentation, and more attempts to have the characters communicate directly with the audience. Oscar Villegas and Willebaldo López, of course, were employing many of these same elements years earlier.

The more recent plays are very different from most of the plays written in the early years of the generation; still, some similarities exist. Those elements in common with the works of Villegas and López are stylistic to a great extent. In a more general sense, the writers continued the criticism of the "system" and all that such criticism entails. The change in point of view away from that of the young shifted the focus of more recent works. The dramatists did not merely see and lament the corruption in society, but tried to understand its causes and its results. The effectiveness in communicating the problems seems to have grown. Unfortunately, though, the hopes for correcting them have not.

9. Conclusion
A Beginning

It can be claimed that the new generation of Mexican drama officially began with Oscar Villegas's publication of *La paz de la buena gente* in 1966. Since he helped inaugurate the period, it seems appropriate that he reappeared in its later years. For twelve years Villegas abandoned playwriting and concentrated on making ceramics, but some of the events mentioned in previous chapters helped lead him back to drama. His style changed very little and, if anything, the base for his material broadened as he continued to express many of the fundamental concerns of the *Nueva Dramaturgia* generation. These concerns are apparent in *Mucho gusto en conocerlo*.

The actions of the play take place in front of a large pyramid, a reminder that the past still has an influence, and a subtle hint about the violence that was a part of those structures and that has a central role in the play. The actions come in a seemingly chaotic set of fragments consisting of elderly people sitting around talking, young lovers separated by the girl's brother, a family dispute, a Princess who falls in love with a "common Indian," a police interrogation, and more. Each set of actions occupies one or more scenes and, at least on the surface, none connects with the others. There is certainly no single plot line. Although some characters have names, many receive numbers or no identification at all. (As in sections of *La paz de la buena gente*, a change of speakers is indicated with a dash.) The play is not about characters, though; Villegas's theme is more expansive than that.

The title, *Mucho gusto en conocerlo,* is a set social phrase used to convey a personal, affable feeling, yet it is used so much that the personal feeling has been lost to a great extent. People say it without thinking. That attitude sets the stage for the play's thematic material, which centers primarily on language and death, but from which such varied subjects as the treatment of Indians, Modernism, Romeo and Juliet, police methods, social criticism, and family relationships constantly emerge. The treatment is as ingenious as the combination of themes.

The police interrogation, for example, begins on a humorous note. A man is digging a hole at midnight and when he finishes he offers something like a prayer to "Señor dueño de la tierra, sueño germinal" (223). Before he can finish the police interrupt him, one of them ordering the standard "hands up," while the other knowingly comments, "Conque soliloquito, eh . . . " (223). The humor becomes tainted with violence as they tie the man to a tree and begin to torture him, demanding information that he obviously does not possess. At one point he denies being a *contrabandista,* and one of the agents informs him, "Eres sospechoso: eso es delito federal" (224). As they continue to torture him, he finally begins to talk, but what comes out is an Indian version of Creation. As he continues to confess Genesis, the police seem content to listen and ask an occasional question. Villegas manages to combine strong criticism of police tactics, unfair treatment of the Indians, an aspect of indigenous culture, violence, and humor in the same scene. This *tour de force* approach characterizes the whole play.

In another sequence, a mother has just sent her daughter out to inform a friend that she (the mother) plans to die that day, when her son returns home demanding his inheritance. The ensuing shouting match leads to suggestions of incest in the family and finally to the boy's strangling the mother. Thus we witness prescience, greed, sexual aberration, youthful rebellion and defiance, a breakdown in family relations, and violence. Violence seems to be the domain of brothers; in another scene a boy and his girlfriend plan to marry, but her brother arrives and kills the boy because he is not fit to be a part of the family. In earlier plays, of course, the part of family villain was played more frequently by the father.

The unacceptable lover—strains of *Romeo and Juliet*—appears in a more extended form in the story of the Princess who sees an Indian in the market and falls in love with him. The relationship is impossible not only because he is beneath her, but also because her station requires that she remain almost a prisoner in the palace: "No debes dar un solo paso fuera de este recinto, salvo que se celebre algún sacrificio humano; sólo una vez al año en la fiesta mayor es requerido que bailes ante el pueblo" (218). As Rubén Darío might say, "La Princesa está triste," and the playful and highly stylized language does at times seem to echo the Modernist period. The Indian is accepted into the family on a kind of provisional basis. He will receive army training to raise him to the proper level, which really means that he will be sent to war to die in battle, thus disposing of the problem without upsetting the daughter directly. Before he leaves he is allowed to spend the night with her, but much to his dismay, all she wants to do is look at him. That apparent lack of interest does not prevent her from running away (and dying) when he leaves for what she finds out is not really basic training.

Despite a continuing series of deaths Villegas prevented the tone from becoming depressing or melodramatic with his use of language. He constantly plays with meanings, sounds (using rhythm and alliteration extensively), and set phrases. A sampling: "No hay datos exactos—extracto—hay extintos en la extremidad existente" (188); "¡Me impaciento fósilmente!" (189); "¡Quiero maldecir algo al respecto!" (191); "Así es la muerte" (192); "Qué hijos, qué higos, qué hipos, / qué hitos, qué hilos . . . " (194). The juxtaposition of the wordplay and the murderous events undercuts not only the meaning of the words but also the seriousness and the violence of the actions. In the play's first twelve pages, most of which are devoted to a conversation among several elderly people, there are no less than eleven deaths. So many people dying so quickly and the exaggeratedly violent energuman who appears at one point make the loss of life more humorous than sad or tragic. After the ninth or tenth death, it becomes meaningless. It is the combination of the meaningless nature of both death and words in general that makes it easy and natural to say to death, "Mucho gusto en conocerlo."

This accepting attitude toward death in a Mexican play is not that surprising, since it was discussed at some length by Octavio Paz in *El laberinto de la soledad*. He explained, "La indiferencia del mexicano ante la muerte se nutre de su indiferencia ante la vida" (52). Alan Riding concurred: "For Mexicans, neither birth nor death is seen to interrupt the continuity of life and neither is considered overly important" (6). However, against the backdrop of pessimism and ever-diminishing hope seen in so many of the plays produced by this generation, the easy acceptance of death takes on other more ominous meanings.

Villegas's pessimistic views coincided with those of his contemporaries, and this effort proves that he remained a leader among the new playwrights with his innovative and broad-based expression of the whole group's primary concerns: the (sorry) state of society, and everyday reality along with its status and function *vis-a-vis* the social organization. The indifference toward death approaches all too closely the pervasive emptiness and nothingness expressed in Olmos's *El brillo de la ausencia* and in Ruiz Mercado's *Pshklmania* and *Como cualquier historia de familia*. It reflects the hopelessness of being in "prisons" such as those portrayed by Agustín and Bandrich in *Círculo vicioso* and *Lecumberri*, in Licona's *Máquina*, and by Rascón Banda in so many of his plays. By accepting death or prison or emptiness, one admits that change or escape is impossible. It is an admission that González Dávila's *fábrica* can and perhaps does exist; that, as Olmos showed, the alternatives to a death-like life may be something worse; that no matter how hard people try, they are doomed to become a part of the problem, as Espinosa suggested; or that the best people can hope to do is to play for the sake and fun of playing, as do so many of Liera's characters.

Given all that, one need not be surprised that a common tendency among these dramatists was to move away from humor and toward violence in their portrayal of society and reality. To one degree or another such a shift can be found in the work of Licona, González Dávila, Olmos, Villegas, and López, not to mention Campesino, whose plays were violent from the start. The general trajectory followed by all of the dramatists in their portrayal of surrounding reality began with a reproduction of reality along with complaints about its unfairness, particularly toward the young. Next, the playwrights expressed a reaction to the social conditions they saw. The reactions ranged from escape to the hope of bringing about change, the conclusion that their reality was simply empty, and attempts to understand why such situations existed. The last led to examinations of the past, as López, Velásquez, and Berman provided.

The origin of these expectations and attitudes can almost certainly be traced to the events at Tlateloco and more generally to what Riding calls "The Social Crisis." He recalled the commitment and the promise inherent in the Revolution, then added, "But the reality is sadly different. More than seventy years after the Revolution, Mexico's social profile is barely distinguishable from countries of the region that have had no revolution" (219). The disillusionment must also have grown from the dramatists' own personal experiences as part of what is very nearly a lost generation of writers who were ignored (the theme of emptiness), who had no control over their destiny as playwrights, and who found themselves confronted by a "theater mafia" that seemed to the writers to be unfair in its practices. It is not surprising, then, that their primary themes run to the problems that exist in Mexico and to the idea that reality is relative and can be re-formed, manipulated, and even created, although generally by others.

The form that their drama takes began, for the most part, as straightforward, realistic portrayals of life and moved to progressively more experimental structures, characters, and language. Structurally, the early plays are predominantly short and usually chronological one-acts, while later works tend to be longer, at times divided into two acts, but more often into a series of fragments. The original teenaged city-dwellers evolved into members of the older generation, historical figures, and country people in places other than Mexico City. The predominantly realistic language continued, but it expanded and featured more stylization, absurdism, and word-play, all of which tend to undermine the linguistic meaning, its communication of a reality, and eventually even the portrayal of reality itself. More frequently than before, the characters direct their comments to the public; this tactic serves to create a substitute for the reality being undermined in the stage actions, one that includes the audience in the process of change posited by many of the plays.

Tones that began as laments and anger eventually evolved into either a sort of guarded hopefulness on the part of those who continued to look for reasons or change, or into almost anguished hopelessness from those who envisioned little or no chance for change or even escape. The generation's works commonly depict characters who lack control and situations in which a prime element is an unstable reality, often accompanied by a critical commentary on social structures: the unfairness and corruption of government and bureaucracy, and the odds against mutually satisfying personal relationships and the possibility of love. This last aspect is reminiscent of *El laberinto de la soledad*, where Paz says, "En nuestro mundo el amor es una experiencia casi inaccesible" (177). More often than not, that is the case in the drama of this generation.

The development of these dramatists can be categorized into three phases. With the exception of works by Olmos, Villegas, and González Dávila, realism dominated during the first wave and the tone was almost universally pessimistic. López began to use history as his subject matter, a tendency picked up later by Velásquez. During the second phase, the lull, most of the original group of dramatists stopped writing plays. Although realism continued to be a staple, González Dávila turned to writing children's plays and Olmos moved more and more toward invented reality. Velásquez looked outside of Mexico City for characters and locations, began to experiment with "geometric" and "cubist" works, and eventually settled into historically-based drama. Dramatists in the third phase, the "second wave," still practiced realism but also explored many other directions. Campesino, Espinosa, Liera, and Schmidhuber, to mention a few, experimented and played with reality, while Olmos seemed to work to eliminate it. Berman and Liera incorporated history and folklore into their plays, and from many other writers— Licona, González Dávila, Olmos, Rascón Banda, Ruiz Mercado —came allusions to the emptiness all around.

These playwrights found themselves disillusioned with the reception accorded their efforts and with the world they saw around them. They protested against those conditions, against the general lack of control, and against the unfairness and corruption that feeds the lack of control. Riding claimed: "The system has in fact never lived without corruption and it would disintegrate or change beyond recognition if it tried to do so . . . Today, corruption enables the system to function, providing the oil that makes the wheels of the bureaucratic machine turn and the glue that seals political alliances" (113-114). Despite that, in play after play there are protests against corruption, seemingly because the negative consequences of its presence outweigh the possible benefits.

The plays provide insights into a still-young generation's view of the spiritual, physical, and mental state of Mexico. The dramatists' cry for change was generally unheeded and even ignored, although in later years at least the public seemed to have noticed that the voice was there. From 1967 they did not really change their basic message; one need only look closely at the early plays by López and Villegas and Villegas's later work. To their voices one can now add those of other writers such as Berman, Liera, Espinosa, González Dávila, and Olmos, members of a generation that grew in numbers, in determination, in variety of expression, and in quality. Perhaps now that they have managed to attract attention, the public will notice that there is a deep concern expressed over the condition of Mexico in these works. Perhaps now audiences will also begin to notice that those concerns are communicated with increasingly more eloquence and imagination in the plays by dramatists who produced Mexico's latest drama.

Appendix A
Works of the Playwrights

This Appendix lists plays chronologically by author. It represents all the works to which I have access, with indications of other plays of which I am aware but which I was unable to find. Each author's entry shows the year of birth (b) when available. Following each work, when available, are the date of composition (c) and the date and place where the work was premiered (p). There are multiple listings in some instances. *Teatro Infantil* and *pastorelas* are not included, since they constitute a different type of theater from what is considered here.

The following abbreviations are used throughout the listings:

E   =   *Escénica: Revista de Teatro de la Universidad Nacional Autónoma de México* (UNAM).
MTJ =   *Más teatro joven*. Ed. Emilio Carballido. Mexico: Editores Mexicanos Unidos, 1982.
R   =   *Repertorio: Revista de Teatro de la Universidad Autónoma de Querétaro*.
T   =   *Tramoya (Cuaderno de Teatro)*. (Universidad Veracruzana).
TJ (I) = *Teatro joven de México*. Ed. Emilio Carballido. Mexico: Editorial Novaro, 1973.
TJ (II) = *Teatro joven de México*. Ed. Emilio Carballido. Mexico: Editores Mexicanos Unidos, 1980.

AGUSTÍN, JOSÉ (b 1944)
Abolición de la propiedad (c 1968; p May 1978, Denver, Colorado). Mexico: Joaquín Mortiz, 1969.
Los atardeceres privilegiados de la prepa seis (c 1969; p May 26, 1970). *TJ (I)* 235-60. *TJ (II)* 199-222.

Círculo vicioso (c 1972; p May 1972, Teatro de la UNAM). Mexico: Joaquín Mortiz, 1974.

ARGUDÍN, ANTONIO (b 1953, Veracruz)
Las peripecias de un costal. TJ (II) 323-43. *T* 13 (1978): 80-100.
Cypris (c 1979). *T* 18 (1980): 18-27.
Sueldo según capacidades. MTJ 57-62.
La manzana. Teatro para adolescentes. Ed. Emilio Carballido. Mexico: Editores Mexicanos Unidos, 1985, 197-202.

ASSAF, JESÚS (b 1950, Covarrubias, Veracruz)
Estoy enamorado de tu hermana. TJ (I) 209-22.

AURA, ALEJANDRO (b 1944, Mexico City)
(All works are in *Salón Calavera, Las visitas, Bang . . . !.* Mexico: Ediciones Océano, 1986.)
Salón Calavera (p 1982). 7-50.
Las visitas. 51-92.
Bang . . . ! 93-144.

BALLESTÉ, ENRIQUE (b 1946, Mexico City)
Mínimo quiere saber. TJ (I) 269-92.

BANDRICH, AGUSTÍN (b. 1939, Los Mochis)
Requiem para Lecumberri. In *Premios PROTEA 1976.* Mexico: Editorial Extemporáneos, 1977, 147-297.
El condor travesti (c 1980). Personal copy.

BERMAN, SABINA (b 1953, Mexico City)
(All works are included in *Teatro de Sabina Berman.* Mexico: Editores Mexicanos Unidos, 1985. Original titles are listed in parentheses after the current title.)
Un actor se repara (*Este no es una obra de teatro*) (c 1975; p 1977 [original version], 1984 [current version]). *Un actor,* 312-23; *Esta no,* 300-311.
El suplicio del placer (*El jardín de las delicias*) (c 1978; p 1978). 266-99.
Yankee (*Bill*) (c 1979; p 1980). 11-56. *Bill. MTJ,* 123-71.
Rompecabezas (*Un buen trabajador del piolet*) (c 1982). 57-145.
Herejía (*Anatema*) (c 1983; p 1984). 147-211.
Aguila o sol (c 1984; p 1985). 223-65.

BERTHIER, HÉCTOR (b 1952, Mexico City)
El corsario negro (p 1976, UNAM). *TJ (II)* 303-21.
Cuentan, entre las cosas que cuentan. Personal copy.

CAMPESINO, PILAR (also PILAR RETES) (b 1945, Mexico City)

Los objetos malos (c 1967).
Verano negro (c 1968; p 1968). *TJ (II)* 249-68.
Octubre terminó hace mucho tiempo (c 1969; p 1971, New York, Community
Center Theater). *MTJ* 199-241. *T* 1-2 (1975): 13-38.
Superocho (c 1979). *T* 20 (1980): 71-104.

CARBALLIDO, REYNALDO (b 1949, Tequisistlán, Oaxaca)

(TR = Tiempos revueltos (1987): Mexico: Instituto Politécnico Nacional.)
Acto social (c 1973; p 1979). *T* 9 (1977): 93-100.
El periódico (c 1973; p 1979). *TR* 53-65. *T* 9 (1977): 86-92.
La señora de gris (c 1973; p 1979). *TR* 67-81. *T* 9 (1977): 76-85.
Los mandamientos de la ley del hombre (c 1974; p 1979). *T* 9 (1977): 101-10.
Moto en delegación (c 1975; p 1979). *T* 9 (1977): 66-75.
La corriente: Obra en tres secuencias (c 1978; p 1980). *TJ (II)* 175-98.
Sombras ajenas (c 1980; p 1981). *MTJ* 43-54. *TR* 83-99. *T* 18 (1980): 49-58.
Nosotros, los de entonces. *TR* 101-18.
Cuestión de prácticas (c 1985). *TR* 13-51.

CRUZ, CASTO EUGENIO (b 1949, Oaxaca)

Taller de ciencias sociales (c 1977). *TJ (II)* 97-104.

DE VELASCO, DOLLY S.

La carretera a Tokaido. In *3 Piezas de Teatro Joven Jalisciense*. Guadalajara:
Departamento de Bellas Artes del Gobierno del Estado, 1975, 7-63.

DEL CASTILLO, DANTE (b 1946, Orizaba, Veracruz)

El desempleo (I) (c 1969). In *Aleluyas para Dos Desempleos y un Tema de
Amor* (Cuatro obras teatrales del Taller de Composición Dramática
del IPN). Mexico: Instituto Politécnico Nacional, 1970, 15-43.
Riesgo, vidrio (c 1970; p 1970). *TJ (I)* 193-208. *MTJ* 243-60.
Las muñecas (c 1971; p 1973, Teatro Tepeyac). In *Muñecas de magia y plata*.
Mexico: Instituto Politécnico Nacional, 1987, 13-83.
El gerente (c 1972). *TJ (II)* 151-63. In *La Palabra y el Hombre* 6 (1973): 60-
72.
Adán, Eva y la otra (c 1976; p 1982). *T* 19 (1980): 67-110.
El prendedor (c 1977). In *El Cuento. Revista de Imaginación* 76 (1977): 323-
30.
Nada que ver una con otra (p 1979). In *El Gallo Ilustrado* (El semanario de
"El Día") 985 (May 3, 1981): 13-17.
Mulata con magia y plata (c 1983). In *Muñecas de magia y plata*. Mexico:
Instituto Politécnico Nacional, 1987, 85-151.

DIAZ MORA, MARGARITA

Juguemos a la verdad.
La mariposa incorruptible (p November 28, 1979, UAM). Mexico: Universidad Autónoma Metropolitana, 1980.

ESPINOSA, TOMÁS (b 1947, Mexico City)

El teléfono. T 16 (1979): 4-12.
Hacer la calle T 16 (1979): 13-21. *MTJ* 173-84.
Angélica y Araceli. T 16 (1979): 22-26.
Ejemplo. T 16 (1979): 27-33.
La rata. T 16 (1979): 34-39.
La televisión enterrada. T 18 (1980): 91-99.
Santísima la nauyaca. T 20 (1980): 5-33.
Los ríos ocultos. In *Danza y Teatro* 7.36 (1982, 1983): 58-61.
La noche de las nictálopes (c 1982; p 1985). Personal copy.
María o la sumisión. Personal copy.

GALVÁN, FELIPE (b 1949, Mexico City)

La historia de Miguel (p 1980). *MTJ* 279-305. *T* 20 (1980): 37-56.

GONZÁLEZ DÁVILA, JESÚS (b 1941, Mexico City)

La rana (c 1968; p 1968). No copy in existence.
La venturina (c 1968; p 1968). No copy in existence.
El camino (c 1969; p 1969). No copy in existence.
La fábrica de los juguetes (c 1970; p 1979, Teatro Gorostiza). *TJ (II)* 65-95. *T* 11 (1978): 62-89.
Polo Pelota Amarilla (c 1978). Personal copy.
Los niños prohibidos (c 1981). In *La Cabra (Revista de Teatro)* 3.38 (1981): III-XVI.
De la calle (c 1983; p 1987). *E* 1.11 (1985): 52-64.
Pastel de zarzamoras (c 1983). In *Trilogía. Tres obras en un acto.* Mexico: Universidad Autónoma de Puebla, 1984, 9-48.
Muchacha del alma (c 1983; p 1985). In *Trilogía. Tres obras en un acto.* Mexico: Universidad Autónoma de Puebla, 1984, 93-137. *E* 1.6-7 (1984): VII-XXIII.
El jardín de las delicias (c 1984; p 1984). In *Trilogía. Tres obras en un acto.* Mexico: Universidad Autónoma de Puebla, 1984, 49-92.

GONZÁLEZ GÓMEZ, MIGUEL

Máscaras (Teatro Poético). Guadalajara: Edición del Ayuntamiento de Guadalajara, 1971-73.

Los monos (Teatro de Eros). Guadalajara: Ediciones del Centro Cultural Universitario Independiente, 1973.

Los geranios blancos. In *SUMMA (Revista de Cultura e Información)* 2.4 (1980): 3-36.

KOSTA KOSTA, LEONARDO

La pata de Santa Anna (c 1982). *R 2.5-6* (1982): 70-128.

LICONA, ALEJANDRO (b 1953, Mexico City)

(RVM = Raptola, violola y matola (1987): Mexico: Instituto Politécnico Nacional, 1987.)

Huélum o Cómo pasar matemáticas sin problema (c 1972; p 1981). *TJ (II)* 269-301.

El diablo en el jardín (c 1977; p 1980). Personal copy.

Cuentas por cobrar (c 1979; p 1985). *MTJ* 31-41. *T* 18 (1980): 28-36.

Máquina (c 1979; p 1980, Los Angeles, Cal.). *T* 19 (1980): 4-50. In *Teatro para obreros.* Ed. Emilio Carballido. Mexico: Editores Mexicanos Unidos, 1985, 55-117.

Esta es su casa (c 1980). *RVM* 84-127.

El capiro (c 1981). In *El Gallo Ilustrado* (Semanario de "El Día") 985 (May 3, 1981): 3.

Cancionero popular (c 1982; p 1982, Mexicali). Personal copy.

La amenaza roja (c 1984). In *Escándalo en Paraíso y 4 obras ganadoras* (Primer Concurso de Teatro Salvador Novo). Mexico: Editores Mexicanos Unidos, 1984, 169-222.

El día de mañana (c 1985). *RVM* 129-39.

LIERA, OSCAR (b 1946, Culiacán, Sinaloa)

(PM = La piña y la manzana. Viejos juegos en la dramática. Mexico: UNAM, 1982.)

Las Ubárry (c 1979). *TJ (II)* 55-64. *PM* 27-35. *T* 14 (1979): 30-37.

El Lazarillo (p June 6, 1979, UAM). Mexico: Universidad Autónoma Metropolitana, 1983.

Cúcara y Mácara (p 1980, Xalapa). In *La Cabra. Revista de Teatro* 3.28-29 (1981): I-XII. *PM* 101-20.

La ñonga. Personal copy.

Gente de teatro, gente horrible. Personal copy.

Las fábulas perversas. Personal copy.

Los fantasmas de la realidad. Personal copy.

La gudógoda T 18 (1980): 77-81.

Etcétera R7 (1982): 1-14.

La fuerza del hombre. PM 7-13. *T* 14 (1979): 23-29. *MTJ* 187-96. In *Teatro breve.* Mexico: Arbol Editorial, 1984, 51-58.
El gordo (p 1980). *PM* 15-25. *T* 14 (1979): 38-48.
Los camaleones (p 1980). *PM* 37-43. *T* 14 (1979): 17-22.
La verdadera revolución. PM 45-47.
El crescencio. PM 49-62. *T* 14 (1979): 4-16.
Aquí no pasa nada. PM 63-77. *T* 14 (1979): 49-62.
La piña y la manzana. PM 79-88. *T* 14 (1979): 63-72.
La pesadilla de una noche de verano. PM 89-100.
Soy el hombre. PM 121-36.
Juego de damas. PM 137-71.
Las juramentaciones. Personal copy.
El oro de la revolución mexicana (c 1984). Personal copy.
Inventario de indulgencias. Personal copy.
Bajo el silencio (c 1984). Personal copy.
El jinete de la divina providencia (c 1984; p July 7, 1984, Culiacán). Culiacán: Universidad Autónoma de Sinaloa, 1987. *E* 1.10 (1985): I-XX.
Un misterioso pacto (c 1985). Personal copy.
El camino rojo a Sabaiba (c 1985). Personal copy.
Los negros pájaros del adios. Personal copy.

LÓPEZ, WILLEBALDO (b 1944, Queréndaro, Michoacán)

Los arrieros con sus burros por la hermosa capital (c 1967; p May, 1967, Teatro Hidalgo). *TJ (I)* 103-39. *TJ (II)* 115-49. Mexico: Ediciones INFONAVIT, 1978.
Cosas de muchachos (c 1968; p 1968, Teatro Jiménez Rueda). *MTJ* 65-102. *T* 1-2 (1975): 39-60. *T* 13 (1978): 4-32. Mexico: Ediciones del Sindicato de Trabajadores del INFONAVIT, 1978.
Vine, vi y mejor me fui (c 1971; p 1975, Festival de Manizales). Mexico: Obra Citada, S.A., 1988.
Yo soy Juárez (c 1972; p 1972, Teatro Independencia). In *Teatro mexicano 1972.* Mexico: Editorial Aguilar, 1975, 31-96.
Pilo Tamirano Luca (c 1973; p. 1972, Teatro Hidalgo). In *Segundo Concurso Nacional de Obras de Teatro: Hombres de México y del Mundo. México: Sus Raíces y su Folklore* 1973, 3-44.
José (c 1975; p 1976, University of California at Berkeley). Personal copy.
Malinche Show (c 1977; p 1977, Teatro de Estado, Mexicali, B.C.). Mexico: Ediciones del Sindicato de Trabajadores del INFONAVIT, 1980.

LÓPEZ ARELLANO, JOSÉ (b 1951, Mexico City)

El soplete. TJ (I) 27-35.
En el hueco de la mano. TJ (II) 45-54.
Otra visión o el nido del amor. T 18 (1980): 83-90.

Diálogo submarino. MTJ 261-77.
Querido diario (p 1982). *T* 24-25 (1982): 12-24.

LUNA, JOSÉ (b 1948, Topotzotlán)
El hacha (p 1970). *TJ (I)* 177-91.

MARÍN, SILVIA (b 1953, Mexico City)
Urgencias (c 1979). *MTJ* 383-97. *T* 18 (1980): 65-76.

OLMOS, CARLOS (b 1947, Chiapas)
(*TDJ* = *Tríptico de juegos.* Mexico: INBA, 1975.)
Juegos fatuos (c 1968; p 1972). *TDJ* 57-109. In *Teatro mexicano 1972.* Mexico:
    Editorial Aguilar, 1975, 159-208.
Juegos impuros (c 1969; p 1974). *TDJ* 46-55.
Lenguas muertas (c 1970; p 1975). *Teatro.* Xalapa: Universidad Veracru-
    zana, 1983, 9-78.
Juegos profanos (c 1970; p 1976). *TDJ* 8-44.
El presente perfecto (c 1975; p 1982). *Teatro.* Xalapa: Universidad Veracru-
    zana, 1983, 79-139. In *El presente perfecto y Las ruinas de Babilonia.*
    Mexico: FONAPAS Chiapas, 1979, 43-106.
Las ruinas de Babilonia (c 1975). In *El presente perfecto y Las ruinas de Ba-
    bilonia.* Mexico: FONAPAS Chiapas, 1979, 9-41.
La rosa de oro (c 1980; p July, 1981). *T* 24-25 (1982): 55-91.
El brillo de la ausencia (c 1982; p 1984). *Teatro.* Xalapa: Universidad Vera-
    cruzana, 1983, 215-90.

PATRICIO, CLAUDIO
Día de graduación. Personal copy.

PEREGRINA, SERGIO (b 1950, Mexico City)
El desempleo (II) (c 1969). In *Aleluyas para Dos Desempleos y un Tema de
    Amor* (Cuatro obras teatrales del Taller de Composición Dramática
    del IPN). Mexico: Instituto Politécnico Nacional, 1970, 65-83. In *Teatro
    para obreros.* Ed. Emilio Carballido. Mexico: Editores Mexicanos Uni-
    dos, 1985, 41-53.
Dolor de muchos (c 1971). Personal copy.
Un tanque parado en un nopal (c 1971). Personal copy.
El cuarto año "A" (c 1972). Personal copy.
Jonás (c 1972). Personal copy.
Dúo de cuatro. Personal copy.
Volver a decir el mar (c 1972). *TJ (I)* 141-47. *TJ (II)* 109-13.
Pater ex máquina Personal copy.
El quinto ángel (c 1972). In *La Palabra y el Hombre* 4 (1972).

La rueda de la fortuna (c 1973). *Revista de Bellas Artes* (1983), 84-88.
Cocina vegetariana (c 1973; p 1977, CADAC). In *Abuelo de Pájaro* (Nueve Obras de Teatro del Taller de Composición Dramática del IPN). Zacatenco: IPN, 1973, 57-67.

RAMÍREZ HEREDIA, RAFAEL (b 1940, Mexico City)
Dentro de estos ocho muros. In *Premios PROTEA 1976.* Mexico: Editorial Extemporáneos, 1977, 7-67.

RASCÓN BANDAS, VÍCTOR HUGO (b 1950, Uruáchic, Chihuahua)
(*TD* = *Teatro del delito.* Mexico: Editores Mexicanos Unidos, 1985.
TM = *Tina Modotti y otras obras de teatro.* Mexico: Secretaría de Educación Pública, 1986.)
Los ilegales (c 1977; p June 1978, UAM). Mexico: Universidad Autónoma Metropolitana, 1980.
Voces en el umbral (c 1977; p November 1984, Chihuahua). Mexico: Universidad Autónoma Metropolitana, 1983. *R* 2.5-6 (1982): 39-69. *TM* 9-48.
La Maestra Teresa (c 1979). Personal copy.
Las armas blancas (c 1980; p Feb. 11, 1982). Personal copy. [*Las armas blancas* includes *El machete, La navaja, La daga,* and *El abrecartas. La daga* appears in *MTJ* 399-428, and in *El Gallo Ilustrado* (El Semanario de "El Día") 985 (May 3, 1981): 7-12.]
Tina Moddotti (c 1980; p April 1983). *TM* 101-73.
El baile de los montañeses (c 1981; p May 1982). Mexico: Universidad Autónoma del Estado de México, 1982.
Playa azul (c 1982). *TM* 49-100.
La fiera del Ajusco (first appeared as *La razón de Elvira*). (c 1983; p Sep. 6, 1985). *Razón* in *R* 2.5-6 (1982): 1-38. *Fiera* in *TD* 109-66.
Manos arriba (c 1983; p March 1984). *TD* 39-107.
Máscara vs. Cabellera (c 1985; p June 15, 1985). *TD* 185-251.

REYES PALACIOS, FELIPE (b 1945, Mexico City)
Los colmillos de la ballena TJ (I) 149-75.
Diálogo entre el enterrador y un zapatero (p 1967). *TJ (II)* 105-8.

RODRÍQUEZ SOLÍS, EDUARDO (b 1938)
Banderitas de papel picado (c 1964).
Las ruedas ruedan (c 1965).
Blackjack (c 1968).
Un encuentro de los agentes secretos. Mexico: Universidad Autónoma Metropolitana, 1982.

RUIZ MERCADO, JOSÉ (b 1954, Guadalajara)

Pshklmania. In *3 Piezas de Teatro Joven Jalisciense*. Guadalajara: Departamento de Bellas Artes del Gobierno del Estado, 1975, 85-108.
Como cualquier historia de familia. *MTJ* 317-44.

RUVALCABA, EUSEBIO (b 1951, Guadalajara)

(*LDC* = *Las dulces compañías*, Mexico: Panfleto y Pantomima, 1984.)
Las dulces compañías T 18 (1980): 59-63. *LDC* 37-43.
La muerte y la doncella (c 1981). Personal copy.
La visita (c 1981). *MTJ* 103-11. *LDC* 9-18. In *El Gallo Ilustrado* (Semanario de "El Día") 985 (May 3, 1981): 5-6.
¡Ahí viene! ¡Ahí viene! (c 1981). *LDC* 19-28.
¿Quién de ustedes ha recorrido el mundo? LDC 29-36.
Bienvenido, papá. LDC 45-53.
La estrella de mar. Personal copy.

SCHMIDHUBER DE LA MORA, GUILLERMO (b 1943, Mexico City)

La parábola de la mala posada (c 1968).
La catedral humana (c 1973-1974; p Nov. 18, 1983, Teatro NOVA, Monterrey). Monterrey: Ediciones Sierra Madre, 1984.
Nuestro Señor Quetzalcoatl (c 1974; p May 18, 1979). Monterrey: Ediciones Sierra Madre, 1979.
La mano del hombre. (c 1977).
Juegos centrífugos (c 1978; p Jan. 27, 1985, Hermosillo). *R* 2 (1982).
Todos somos el Rey Lear (c 1979). *Teatro*. Monterrey, Mexico: Ediciones Cerda, 1982, 41-72.
Los héroes inútiles (c 1979; p August 7, 1980, Monterrey). *Teatro*. Monterrey, Mexico: Ediciones Cerda, 1982, 5-39.
Los herederos de Segismundo (c 1980; p April 28, 1981, Guanajuato). Mexico: Editorial FONAPAS, 1982. Mexico: Ediciones Oasis, 1985.
El robo del penacho de Moctezuma (c 1981; p May 10, 1985, Monterrey). *R* 4 (1982).
Lacandonia (c 1982). *Teatro*. Monterrey, Mexico: Ediciones Cerda, 1982, 73-123.
Cuarteto de mi gentedad (c 1983). Mexico: Ediciones Oasis, 1985. Contains *Perros bravos, Fuegos truncos, La ventana*, and *María Terrones*.
Perros bravos (c 1980; p 1982, Caracas), 85-105. *R* 2 (1982).
Fuegos truncos (c 1982; p Monterrey), 7-34. In *Fuego: Valores Contemporáneos*, Cerillera La Central, 1984.
La ventana (c 1983; p Mérida), 55-83.
María Terrones (c 1983; p May 10, 1986, Monterrey), 35-54. In *Estaciones* 1.1 (Casa de la Cultura de Monterrey), 1984.

Felicidad Instantánea—Instant Happiness (c 1983; p Oct. 4, 1985, Monterrey). Mexico: Ediciones Cerda, 1983.
El día que Monalisa dejó de sonreir (c 1985; p Aug. 15, 1988, Cincinnati). Mexico: Ediciones Oasis, 1987.
Por las tierras de Colón (c 1986; p May 3, 1989; Southwestern College, Chula Vista). Mexico: "Periódico El Porvenir," Monterrey, 1987. Spain: Salvat, 1988. Chile: Ediciones LAR, 1988.
El cíclope (c 1987).

SÁNCHEZ FÉLIX, C. HIRAM (b 1942, Navojoa, Sonora)
El perfil del aire. Guadalajara, 1973.

TÉLLEZ, LETICIA (b 1952, Mexico City)
La tercera ley de Newton (p June 1970). *TJ (I)* 223-33. *TJ (II)* 165-74.

TENORIO, MIGUEL ÁNGEL (b 1954, Mexico City)
(*ESR = Era solo rock 'n roll.* Mexico: Instituto Politécnico Nacional, 1987.)
¡Adios, Malena! (c 1971; p 1974, Instituto Politécnico Nacional). Personal copy.
La botana (c 1971; p 1975, Escuela Normal Superior). In *Juego de Palabras* 2, IPN.
El paletero tenía la razón (c 1971; p 1975, Escuela Normal Superior). *TJ (I)* 261-68.
Fe (c 1972). In *Abuelo de Pájaro* (Nueve obras de teatro del Taller de Composición Dramática del IPN). Zacatenco: IPN, 1973.
Naufragio (c 1972). Personal copy.
Cambio de valencia o el espíritu de la lucha (c 1975; p Nov. 13, 1975, Teatro Celestino Gorostiza). *TJ (II)* 223-48. In *Punto de Partida* 49-50: 137-51.
Cosas del oficio (c 1975). Personal copy.
Sin respuesta (c 1975). In *El Gallo Ilustrado* (Semanario de "El Día") 985 (May 3, 1981): 4.
En español se dice "abismo" (c 1975; p 1979). *MTJ* 345-82.
De naufragios y otras miserias (c 1977). *ESR* 65-141.
El día que Javier se puso águila (c 1978). *T* 10 (1978): 13-48.
Colgar la vida (c 1984). *ESR* 11-64.

TOVAR, JUAN (b 1941, Puebla)
Markheim. TJ (I) 37-49.

ULLOA CÁRDENAS, CONRADO
Maldita inquisición. In *3 Piezas de Teatro Joven Jalisciense.* Guadalajara: Departamento de Bellas Artes del Gobierno del Estado, 1975, 65-83.

VALENZUELA, TERESA (b 1951, Irapuato)
Estela o la geografía política. MTJ 307-15.
Dijeron que a todos. In *Teatro para obreros.* Ed. Emilio Carballido. Mexico: Editores Mexicanos Unidos, 1985, 127-35.

VARGAS, FÉLIX (b 1943)
Las dos soledades (c 1975; p April 18, 1979, Teatro Experimental de Jalisco). Personal copy.
Jesús, María, y José (c 1979; p 1982). Guadalajara: Universidad de Guadalajara, 1984.
La casa de los caballos muertos. Guadalajara: Universidad de Guadalajara, 1979.

VELÁSQUEZ, GERARDO (b 1949, Cárdenas, San Luis Potosí)
(*RH = Rubor helado.* Mexico: Instituto Politécnico Nacional, 1987.)
Ahí vienen los aleluyas (c 1969; p 1970, Teatro Politécnico). In *Aleluyas para Dos Desempleos y un Tema de Amor* (Cuatro obras del Taller de Composición Dramática del IPN). Mexico: IPN, 1970, 85-125. *TJ (I)* 51-75.
Chana volante o la jaula de los canarios (c 1973). *T* 4 (1976): 28-37. In *El Cuento* (Jan.-Feb. 1977).
El cuarto más tranquilo (c 1974; p 1975). *T* 4 (1976): 10-18. *RH* 63-74. In *Punto de Partida* 49-50.
En "El Gato Negro" (c 1974; p 1978). *T* 4 (1976): 18-28.
Las viudas (c 1974). *RH* 81-90.
Agua de limón (c 1974; p 1977). *T* 4 (1976): 37-49.
Amapola (c 1974). *T* 4 (1976): 49-60.
Una ciudad grande y lejana (c 1975). *T* 4 (1976): 72-84.
Un patio a oscuras (c 1976). *T* 4 (1976): 61-72.
La huerta (c 1976). Personal copy.
Toño Basura (c 1977). Personal copy.
Los cuentos del gato encaramado (c 1977). Personal copy.
Sobre las lunas (c 1978; p 1979). *RH* 91-131.
Vía libre (c 1979). *RH* 19-61. In *Punto de Partida* 68-69 (1980): 56-90.
Hasta hacernos polvo juntos (c 1980). *RH* 75-80.
Aunque vengas en figura distinta, Victoriano Huerta (c 1983). Mexico: INBA and Editorial Katún, 1985.

VILLEGAS, OSCAR (b 1943, Ciudad del Maíz, San Luis Potosí)
(*MG = Mucho gusto en conocerlo y otras obras.* Mexico: Editores Mexicanos Unidos, 1985.)
La paz de la buena gente (c 1966; p 1980). *MG* 9-50. In *Revista de Bellas Artes* 18 (1967): 49-64.

El renacimiento (c 1967; p 1971, Xalapa). *TJ (II)* 11-30. In *La Palabra y el Hombre* 44 (1967): 795-835.

El señor y la señora (c 1967; p 1979). In *El señor y la señora y Marlon Brando es otro*. Mexico: Instituto Nacional de la Juventud Mexicana, 1969, 3-43.

La pira (c 1967; p May 1970, Teatro El Grillo, Monterrey). *MTJ* 11-41. *T* 9 (1977): 4-21. In *Juego de Palabras* (Revista de los Talleres Literarios del Instituto Politécnico Nacional) 3 (1972): 26-33.

Marlon Brando es otro (c 1967; p 1977). *TJ (I)* 19-26. In *El señor y la señora y Marlon Brando es otro*. Mexico: Instituto Nacional de la Juventud Mexicana, 1969.

Santa Catarina (c 1969; p 1980). *MG* 51-109. In *Premios PROTEA 1976*. Mexico: Editorial Extemporáneos, 1977, 69-146.

Atlántida (c 1973; p 1976, Xalapa). *MG* 111-84. *T* 2 (1976): 28-86.

El reino animal (c 1964). *T*23 (1982): 108-15.

Mucho gusto en conocerlo (c 1981). *MG* 185-247.

Appendix B
Plays in the
Nueva Dramaturgia
Series

This section lists the thirty-five works presented in the *Nueva Dramaturgia Mexicana* series from 1979 to 1982, followed by the "Lecturas" held in 1981 and 1982.

1. Esteban Cruz, *Historia de hospital*; Dir: Esteban Cruz; Estreno 28 febrero 1979; Unidad Azcapotzalco.

2. Reynaldo Carballido, *El periódico*; Dir: Valentina Hernández; Estreno 7 marzo 1979; Unidad Azcapotzalco.

3. Sergio Peregrina, *Cocina vegetariana*; Dir: Valentina Hernández; Estreno 7 marzo 1979, Unidad Azcapotzalco.

4. Gerardo Velásquez, *Chana volante*; Dir: Valentina Hernández; Estreno 7 marzo 1979; Unidad Azcapotzalco.

5. Sabina Berman, *El jardín de las delicias*; Dir: Teresa Valdez; Estreno 21 marzo 1979; Unidad Azcapotzalco.

6. Gerardo Velásquez, *Sobre las lunas*; Dir: Héctor Berthier; Estreno 28 marzo 1979; Unidad Azcapotzalco.

7. Reynaldo Carballido, *Moto en delegación*; Dir: Jorge Galván; Escenografía: Jorge Galván; Estreno 16 mayo 1979, Unidad Azcapotzalco.

8. Reynaldo Carballido, *Acto social*; Dir: Jorge Galván; Escenografía: Jorge Galván; Estreno 16 mayo 1979; Unidad Azcapotzalco.

9. Reynaldo Carballido, *La señora de gris*; Dir: Jorge Galván; Escenografía: Jorge Galván; Estreno 16 mayo 1979; Unidad Azcapotzalco.

10. Reynaldo Carballido, *Los mandamientos de la ley del hombre*; Dir: Jorge Galván; Escenografía: Jorge Galván; Estreno 16 mayo 1979; Unidad Azcapotzalco.

11. Abraham Caballero Arzate, *Pobre madre mía*; Dir: Mario Ficachi; Estreno 23 mayo 1979; Unidad Azcapotzalco.

12. Oscar Liera, *El lazarillo*; Dir: Oscar Liera; Coreografía: Onésimo González; Música: Alicia Urreta; Estreno 6 junio 1979; Unidad Azcapotzalco.

13. Ricardo Ramírez Carnero, *Un hogar como cualquier otro*; Dir: Ignacio Sotelo; Escenografía: Marcela Zorrilla; Estreno 6 junio 1979; Teatro Ricardo Flores Magón.

14. Víctor Hugo Rascón Banda, *Los ilegales*; Dir: Marta Luna; Escenografía: Ramiro Sotelo; Estreno 19 julio 1979; Auditoria SAHOP.

15. Dante del Castillo, *Nada que ver una con otra*; Dir: Dante del Castillo; Coreografía: Guillermo Serret Bravo; Estreno 27 julio 1979; Unidad Azcapotzalco.

16. Miguel Angel Tenorio, *En español se dice abismo*; Dir: Dante del Castillo; Escenografía: Rosalba del Castillo; Estreno 7 noviembre 1979; Unidad Azcapotzalco.

17. Eduardo Rodríguez Solís, *069 reportándose*; Dir: Eduardo Rodríguez Solís; Estreno 14 noviembre 1979; Unidad Azcapotzalco.

18. Sofía Rodríguez Fernández, *El reloj*; Dir: Sofía Rodríguez Fernández; Escenografía: Fernando Vázquez Mendoza; Estreno 21 noviembre 1979; Unidad Azcapotzalco.

19. Carlos López Beltrán, *Seis cordiales minutos*; Dir: Fernando Vázquez Mendoza; Estreno 21 noviembre 1979; Unidad Azcapotzalco.

20. Sofía Rodríguez Fernández, *Olor a primavera*; Dir: Horacio Romero; Escenografía: Fernando Vázquez Mendoza; Estreno 21 noviembre 1979; Unidad Azcapotzalco.

21. Sofía Rodríguez Fernández, *Amor perdido*; Dir: Raquel Peredo; Escenografía: Fernando Vázquez Mendoza; Estreno 21 noviembre 1979; Unidad Azcapotzalco.

22. Carmen Torres, *En familia*; Dir: Colectiva; Escenografía: Fernando Vázquez Mendoza; Estreno 21 noviembre 1979; Unidad Azcapotzalco.

23. Margarita Díaz Mora, *La mariposa incorruptible*; Dir: Marta Luna; Estreno 28 noviembre 1979; Unidad Azcapotzalco.

24. Antonio Argudín, *Las peripecias de un costal o la corona de hierro*; Dir: Ignacio Sotelo y Manuel Aguilar; Estreno 5 diciembre 1979; Teatro Ricardo Flores Magón.

25. Alejandro Licona, *Máquina*; Dir: Marta Luna; Escenografía: Gloria Olivares; Coreografía: Guillermo Serret Bravo; Música: Larry Borden; Estreno 25 junio 1980; Unidad Azcapotzalco.

26. Reynaldo Carballido, *La corriente*; Dir: Mercedes de la Cruz; Coreografía: Carlos Gaona; Estreno 4 septiembre 1980; Teatro Ricardo Flores Magón.

27. Oscar Villegas, *La paz de la buena gente*; Dir: Emilio Carballido; Escenografía: Jarmila Masserova; Coreografía: Rosa Reyna; Música: Rafael Elizondo; Estreno 6 noviembre 1980; Teatro Ricardo Flores Magón. Reposición 7 enero 1981; Teatro Celestino Gorostiza.

28. Alejandro Licona, *Huélum, o cómo pasar matemáticas sin problema*; Dir: Emilio Carballido; Escenografía: Henry Hagan; Coreografía: Guillermina Bravo; Estreno 13 marzo 1981; Teatro Celestino Gorostiza.

29. Otto Minera, *Siete pecados en la capital*; Dir: Paco Giménez; Escenografía: Juan José Barreiro; Coreografía: Marigely A. Crespo y Norma Angélica; Música: Jorge Jufresa, Quezadas, Jesús Echeverria y Roberto Morales; Estreno 1 junio 1981; Teatro Celestino Gorostiza.

30. Felipe Santander, *A propósito de Ramona*; Dir: Felipe Santander; Escenografía: Mario Orozco Rivera; Música: Roberto y Rodrigo Morales; Estreno 4 agosto 1981; Teatro el Galeón.

31. Hugo Hiriart, *La Ginecomaquia*; Dir: José Caballero; Escenografía: Nazario Martínez; Estreno 15 octubre 1981; Teatro Coyoacán.

32. Carlos Olmos, *El presente perfecto*; Dir: Soledad Ruiz; Escenografía y Vestuario: Miguel Couturier; Estreno 20 febrero 1982; Teatro Celestino Gorostiza.

33. Felipe Galván, *La historia de Miguel*; Dir: Héctor del Puerto; Escenografía y Vestuario: Jarmila Masserova; Música: Joaquín López Chapman; Estreno 3 junio 1982; Teatro Celestino Gorostiza.

34. Dante del Castillo, *Adán, Eva y la Otra*; Dir: Erika Mireles; Escenografía: Jorge Reyna; Coreografía: Antonio Viveros; Diseño del vestuario: Andrzej Wlodarczyk; Música: Grupo Contraste; Estreno 29 septiembre 1982; Teatro Celestino Gorostiza.

35. Alejandro Aura, *Salón Calavera*; Dir: Alejandro Aura; Escenografía: Octavio Vázquez; Coreografía: Margarita Isabel; Música: Alicia Urreta; Estreno 16 octubre 1982; Teatro Coyoacán.

PRIMER CICLO DE LECTURAS

22 junio 1981	Felipe Galván. "La historia de Miguel." Dirección: Emilio Carballido.
29 junio 1981	Víctor Hugo Rascón Banda. "La daga." Dirección: José Luis Cruz.
13 julio 1981	Oscar Liera. "Las juramentaciones." Dirección: Rogelio Luévano.

20 julio 1981	José Ramón Enríquez. "Una ciudad sin sueño." Dirección: José Caballero.
27 julio 1981	Raúl Torres. "Antología de un vago." Dirección: Erika Mireles.

SEGUNDO CICLO DE LECTURAS

5 octubre 1981	Guillermo Schmidhuber. "El robo del penacho de Moctezuma." Dirección: Valentina Hernández.
19 octubre 1981	Carlos Olmos. "El presente perfecto." Dirección: Soledad Ruiz.
26 octubre 1981	Juan Tovar. "Las adoraciones." Dirección: José Caballero.
9 noviembre 1981	Ricardo Ramírez Carnero. "Otro país." Dirección: Antonio Algarra.
16 noviembre 1981	Hugo Hiriart. "Casandra." Dirección: Mercedes de la Cruz.

TERCER CICLO DE LECTURAS

22 marzo 1982	Efrén Hernández. "Casi sin rozar el mundo." Dirección: Emilio Carballido.
29 marzo 1982	Manuel Herrera. "Programa de sorpresas." Dirección: Dagoberto Guillaumin.
5 abril 1982	Alejandro Aura. "Salón Calavera." Dirección: Alejandro Aura. Música original: Alicia Urreta.
12 abril 1982	Jorge Galván. "Requiem por una esperanza." Dirección: Héctor del Puerto.
19 abril 1982	Luisa Josefina Hernández. "La calle de la gran ocasión." Dirección: Mercedes de la Cruz.

CUARTO CICLO DE LECTURAS

28 junio 1982	Dante del Castillo. "Adán, Eva y la otra." Dirección: Erika Mireles.
5 julio 1982	Claudio Patricio. "Día de graduación." Dirección: José Cortés.
12 julio 1982	José López Arellano. "Querido diario." Dirección: Mercedes de la Cruz.
19 julio 1982	Altaír Tejeda. "Yerbabuena." Dirección: Ricardo Ramírez Carnero.
26 julio 1982	Francisco Monterde. "El presente involuntario." Dirección: José Caballero.

Notes

1. Introduction

1. The numbers and percentages represent an estimate based on the 215 plays that I have managed to collect. This number can be considered nearly complete, and it is certainly a representative sample. It should also be noted that, in many cases, dates are difficult to verify. The date given may vary at times from the date written, to the date published, to the date staged. If more than one date is available, they are considered in that order, putting primary emphasis on the date of composition. See Appendix A for a complete list of plays and dates.

2. The Early Years

1. The plays are *Abolición de la propiedad* and *Círculo vicioso*. They are discussed in the next chapter.

2. In a later version of the play Villegas changed the boys' names, and while the clues to their identity and influence are still present, their detection is more difficult.

3. See the *Arizona Gazette* of 12 November 1966.

4. In the original version of the play Virginia's plan at the end was to go to Acapulco in search of stardom. Even that flicker of idealistic hope disappears in the version published in *Mucho gusto en conocerlo y otras obras*, the Villegas anthology.

5. For comments concerning this phenomenon, see John Brushwood's *La novela mexicana (1967–1982)*, especially pages 17–33.

3. The Generation Gap

1. There is a direct reference to Tlatelolco in Pilar Campesino's *Octubre terminó hace mucho tiempo* and more indirect ones in Jesús González

Dávila's *La fábrica de los juguetes* and in his three plays in *Trilogía*. It is also mentioned in *Día de graduación*, by Claudio Patricio.

4. A Five-Year Lull

1. As always, these figures are based on the plays I have been able to collect; they are approximate, but reasonably accurate.

2. The characteristics presented here are a compilation of common elements mention in Apollinaire, Fry, Gleizes and Metzinger, Golding, and Gray.

5. The Storm Surrounding the Lull

1. The three plays in the anthology are linked by their characters, specifically two of the children in *Pastel de zarzamoras*. The daughter who has run away is the protagonist of *Muchacha del alma*; the rebellious son appears in *El jardín de las delicias*.

7. Spotlight on Society

1. The play is also in the collection *La piña y la manzana*, but the source used here, *Teatro joven de México*, is more easily accessible.

2. More detailed descriptions of the attack appear in almost every Mexico City paper of 30 June 1981. See also Saborit.

3. For the history of the Virgin of Guadalupe, see the representative works by López Beltrán, Martí, and Pompa y Pompa.

4. See also Rius Facius.

5. The play first appeared in *La Cabra* early in 1981. It appeared again the following year in *La piña y la manzana*, a collection of short plays by Liera. Since *La Cabra* is even more difficult to obtain than *La piña y la manzana*, the latter is used here.

6. For a basic explanation of Saussure's theory, see Scholes, 13-22. The diagram is based to some extent on Roman Jakobson's communication diagram. Again, see Scholes, 22-40.

8. Bridging the Gap

1. Although Rodríguez Solís predates the generation, the "Nueva Dramaturgia" series published one of his plays. That is the work included here.

Bibliography

This bibliography contains works cited, works consulted, and generally useful works. It does not contain plays by the authors, since those are listed in Appendix A.

Abel, Lionel. 1963. *Metatheatre: A New View of Dramatic Form*. New York: Hill and Wang.

Alfaro, Marco Antonio. 1981. "Una Salvaje Agresión a Actores." *Esto*, (June 30): 21.

Apollinaire, Guillaume. 1949. *The Cubist Painters: Aesthetic Meditations*. Trans. Lionel Abel. New York: Wittenborn, Shultz, Inc.

Argudín, Yolanda. 1985. *Historia del teatro en México: Desde los rituales prehispánicos hasta el arte dramático de nuestros días*. Mexico: Panorama Editorial.

Arrom, José Juan. 1963. *Esquema generacional de las letras hispanoamericanas*. Bogotá: Instituto Caro y Cuervo.

Artaud, Antonin. 1958. *The Theater and Its Double*. New York: Grove Press.

Azparren Giménez, Leonardo. 1986. "El teatro venezolano en una encrucijada." *Latin American Theatre Review* 20.1: 79-84.

Barthes, Roland. 1974. *S/Z*. Trans. Richard Miller. New York: Hill and Wang.

Brockett, Oscar G. 1974. *The Theatre: An Introduction*. New York: Holt, Rinehart, and Winston.

Bruce-Novoa. 1974. "*Abolición de la propiedad*: Mexican Experimental Theatre." *Latin American Theatre Review* 8.1: 5-9.

Brushwood, John. 1984. *La novela mexicana (1967-1982)*. Mexico City: Grijalbo.

Burgess, Ronald D. 1981. "Gerardo Velásquez: Pieces of the Puzzle." *Latin American Literary Review* 9.19: 17-30.

————. 1981."Willebaldo López: Mexico on Stage." *Latin American Theatre Review* 14.2: 27-39.

————. 1982. "Social Criticism from the Stage: The Concerns of Current Mexican Dramatists." *SECOLAS Annals* 13: 48-56.

————. 1985. "Appearances: The Sub-Versions of *Cúcara y Mácara*." *Chasqui* 15.1: 3-10.

————. 1985. "Importantes avances para la nueva dramaturgia mexicana." *Latin American Theatre Review* 18.1: 97-99.

————. 1985. "El nuevo teatro mexicano y la generación perdida." *Latin American Theatre Review* 18.2: 93-99.

————. 1987. "Sabina Berman's Art of Creative Failure: *Bill*." *Gestos* 2.3: 103-13.

Campbell, Joseph. 1949. *The Hero with a Thousand Faces*. Princeton: Princeton University Press.

Carballido, Emilio. 1975. "Cosas de muchachos de octubre." *Tramoya* 1-2: 11.

————, ed. 1973. *Teatro joven de México*. Mexico: Organización Editorial Novaro. Introduction.

————. 1979. "El teatro mexicano." *Revista Mexicana de Cultura, El Nacional*, 4 (Nov. 18). (An interview with Sandra Altamirano.)

————, ed. 1979. *Teatro joven de México*. Mexico: Editores Mexicanos Unidos. Introduction.

————, ed. 1982. *Más teatro joven*. Mexico: Editores Mexicanos Unidos. Introduction

Connell, Dorothy. 1982. "Theatre of Violence." *Index on Censorship* 2.2: 36-37.

Culler, Jonathan. 1975. *Structuralist Poetics*. Ithaca: Cornell University Press.

Danza y teatro. 1982/83, 7.36.

D'Aquino Rosas, Renato. 1981. "Repudian Xalapeños la Obra 'Cúcara y Mácara.' " *El Sol de Xalapa* (January 28).

Dauster, Frank N. 1973. *Historia del teatro hispanoamericano: Siglos XIX y XX*. Mexico: Ediciones de Andrea.

"Demystifying Mexico." 1982. *Index on Censorship* 2.2: 37.

Diez Borque, José María. 1975 "Aproximación semiológica a la 'escena' del teatro del Siglo de Oro español." In *Semiología del teatro*, edited by José María Diez Borque and Luciano García Lorenzo, 49-92. Barcelona: Editorial Planeta.

Erikson, Erik H. 1977. *Toys and Reasons. Stages in the Ritualization of Experience*. New York: W.W. Norton and Company, Inc.

Esslin, Martin. 1969. *The Theatre of the Absurd*. Garden City: Anchor Books.

Fry, Edward F. 1966. *Cubism*. New York: McGraw-Hill.

Gleizes, Albert, and Jean Metzinger. n.d. *Du Cubism*. Paris Eugene Giguière et Cie.

Golding, John. 1968. *Cubism: A History and an Analysis, 1907-1914*. London: Faber and Faber Ltd.

Gray, Christopher. 1953. *Cubist Aesthetic Theories*. Baltimore: The Johns Hopkins Press.

Hawkes, Terence. 1977. *Structuralism and Semiotics*. Berkeley: University of California Press.

Heilman, Robert. 1968. "Tragedy and Melodrama: Speculations on Generic Form." In *Perspectives on Drama*, edited by James L. Calderwood and Harold E. Tolliver, 148-62. New York: Oxford University Press.

Lamb, Ruth and Antonio Magaña Esquivel. 1958. *Breve historia del teatro mexicano*. Mexico: Ediciones de Andrea.

López Beltrán, Lauro. 1966. *La protohistoria guadalupana*. Mexico: Editorial Jus.

Magaña-Esquivel, Antonio. 1964. *Medio siglo de teatro mexicano: 1900-1961*. Mexico: Instituto Nacional de Bellas Artes.

———, ed. 1970. *Teatro mexicano del siglo XX 98*. Mexico: Fondo de Cultura Económica. Introduction.

———, ed. 1970. *Teatro mexicano del siglo XX 99*. Mexico: Fondo de Cultura Económica, 1970. Introduction.

———. 1979. "El teatro mexicano en acción." *Revista Mexicana de Cultura, El Nacional*, 7 (Nov. 18).

———. 1979. "La nueva dramaturgia mexicana." *Revista Mexicana de Cultura, El Nacional*, 7 (Dec. 16).

Martí, Samuel. 1973. *La Virgen de Guadalupe y Juan Diego—The Virgin of Guadalupe and Juan Diego*. Mexico: Ediciones Euroamericanas.

Mendoza López, Margarita. 1985. *Primeros renovadores del teatro en México: 1928-1941*. Mexico: Instituto Mexicano del Seguro Social.

Mendoza López, Margarita, Tomás Espinosa, Daniel Salazar. 1987. *Teatro mexicano del siglo XX 1900-1986. Catálogo de obras teatrales* (2 volumes). Mexico: Instituto Mexicano del Seguro Social.

Moctezuma, Aquiles P. 1960. *El Conflicto Religioso de 1926: Sus Orígenes. Su Desarrollo. Su Solución*. Mexico: Editorial Jus.

Montes Huidobro, Matías. 1982. "Bestiario y metamorfosis en *Santísima la nauyaca* de Tomás Espinosa." *Latin American Theatre Review* 16.1: 41-51.

Morris, Robert J. 1980. "Theatre and Politics in Contemporary Peru." *Latin American Theatre Review* 13.2 (Supplement): 59-62.

Mosley, Nicholas. 1972. *The Assassination of Trotsky*. Great Britain: Josef Shaftel Productions.

Ortega y Gasset, José. 1923. *El tema de nuestro tiempo*. Madrid: Calpe.
———. 1951. *En torno a Galileo*. In *Obras completas* 5: 9-164. Madrid:
    Revista de Occidente.
Otero, Leonardo. 1970. "José Agustín: monólogo e infinito." *Revista de
    la universidad de México*, 24.5-6, suplemento: 11.
Pacheco, Carlos. 1989. " 'La Movida' en Buenos Aires." *Latin American
    Theatre Review* 22.2: 121-24.
Paz, Octavio. 1959. *El laberinto de la soledad*. Mexico: Fondo de Cultura
    Económica.
Pompa y Pompa, Antonio. 1967. *El gran acontecimiento guadalupano*.
    Mexico: Editorial Jus.
Pross, Edith E. 1984. "Open Theatre Revisited: An Argentine Experi-
    ment." *Latin American Theatre Review* 18.1: 83-94.
¿Qué pasa con el teatro en México? 1967. Mexico: Editorial Novaro.
Rabell, Malkah. 1986. *Descenio de teatro 1975-1985*. Mexico: Sociedad
    Cooperativa Publicaciones Mexicanas, S.C.L.
Ramos-Perea, Roberto. 1986. "Nueva dramaturgia puertorriqueña."
    Latin American Theatre Review 20.1: 61-70.
Riding, Alan. 1985. *Distant Neighbors: A Portrait of the Mexicans*. New
    York: Alfred A. Knopf.
Rius Facius, Antonio. 1963. *La Juventud Católica y la Revolución Mexicana:
    1910-1925*. Mexico: Editorial Jus.
Rizk, Beatriz J. 1987. *El nuevo teatro latinoamericano: Una lectura histórica*.
    Minneapolis: The Prisma Institute.
Saborit, Antonio. 1981. "Crónica de una Intolerancia Armada." *Siempre*
    (July 22): 5-10.
Scholes, Robert. 1974. *Structuralism in Literature—An Introduction*. New
    Haven: Yale University Press.
Serge, Victor, and Natalia Sedova Trotsky. 1973. *The Life and Death of
    Leon Trotsky*. Trans. Arnold J. Pomerans. N.Y.: Basic Books, Inc.
Sherman, William L. and Richard E. Greenleaf. 1960. *Victoriano Huerta:
    A Reappraisal*. Mexico: Mexico City College Press.
Shklovsky, Victor. 1965. "Art as Technique." In *Russian Formalist Criti-
    cism: Four Essays*, edited by Lee T. Lemon and Marion J. Reis, 3-24.
    Lincoln: University of Nebraska Press.
Solórzano, Carlos. 1964. *Teatro latinoamericano en el siglo XX*. Mexico:
    Editorial Pormaca.
———, ed. 1973. *Testimonios teatrales de México*. Mexico: Universidad
    Nacional Autónoma de México. Introduction.
Todorov, Tzvetan. 1977. *The Poetic of Prose*. Trans. Richard Howard.
    Ithaca: Cornell University Press.
Toro, Alfonso. 1944. *La familia Carvajal*. Mexico: Editorial Patria.

Weiss, Peter. 1972. *Trotsky in Exile*. Trans. Geoffrey Skelton. New York: Atheneum.

Wheelwright, Philip. 1962. *Metaphor and Reality*. Bloomington: Indiana University Press.

White, Hayden. 1978. *Tropics of Discourse. Essays in Cultural Criticism*. Baltimore: Johns Hopkins University Press.

Wittig, Susan. 1974. "Toward a Semiotic Theory of the Drama." *Educational Theatre Journal* 26.4: 441-54.

Woodyard, George. 1980. "Language and Tensions in José Agustín's Theater." *Hispania* 63.1: 31-37.

————. 1978. "El teatro de Oscar Villegas: Experimentación con la forma." *Texto Crítico* 4.10: 32-41.

Index

Gramley Library
Salem College
Winston-Salem, NC 27108